Latest Readings

Clive James

Latest Readings

Yale

UNIVERSITY PRESS

New Haven and London

Yale University Press books may be purchased in quantity for
educational, business, or promotional use. For information, please
e-mail sales.press@yale.edu (U.S. office) or sales@yaleup.co.uk
(U.K. office).

Designed by Sonia L. Shannon
Set in Fournier type by Integrated Publishing Solutions,
Grand Rapids, Michigan.
Printed in the United States of America.

Library of Congress Control Number: 2014958943
ISBN 978-0-300-21319-5 (cloth : alk. paper)

A catalogue record for this book is available from the British
Library.

This paper meets the requirements of ANSI/NISO Z39.48-1992
(Permanence of Paper).

10 9 8 7 6 5 4 3 2 1

To my doctors and nurses
at Addenbrooke's Hospital, Cambridge, UK

cras mihi

Contents

Contents

Acknowledgments

MY THANKS TO Prue Shaw, David Free, Claerwen James, and Deirdre Serjeantson for reading the manuscript. The last two I hold responsible for getting me hooked on Patrick O'Brian. Thinking I already knew something, I was always reminded that there was more to know when I conversed with Michael Tanner over coffee after one of our many chance encounters at Hugh's bookstall in the Market Square of Cambridge. Finally I should thank Hugh himself, a quiet man who patiently listened when I extolled the virtues of Flann O'Brien. Meanwhile, Hugh was quietly assessing whether I had enough strength to take a vast book of Modigliani's drawings home by taxi, or whether he should deliver it himself at the end of the day.

Latest Readings

Introduction

WHEN I EMERGED from hospital in early 2010 with a certificate to say that I had a case of leukemia to go with my wrecked lungs, I could hear the clock ticking, and I wondered whether it was worth reading anything both new and substantial, or even rereading something substantial that I already knew about. Poetry, yes: I was putting the finishing touches to my *Poetry Notebook*, and there were still some more notes demanding to be added. But even the slightest book of prose looked like a big thing that I might not have time to get through. The cure for that attitude was Boswell's *Life of Johnson*. After reading the whole masterpiece with delight—I had read bits of it before, but I could now see that it needs to be taken complete —I resolved to get back to Johnson himself later.

In view of the fact that I was once again on my feet, instead of flat on my back, the concept of "later" suddenly seemed less quixotic than realistic. If you don't know the exact moment when the lights will go out, you might as well read until they do. My family's plans for my remaining years of existence included extracting me from my place of work in London and installing my library in a house of its own in Cambridge. In this house I would live, read, and perhaps even write. The move took what seemed like years. About half my books had to be sold off just to create some breathing space. What was left filled the specially built shelves to the limit. I made a vow to myself and all concerned that my book-buying days were over. But with the renewed urge to read, I found, came a renewed urge to buy. In recent years the number of secondhand bookshops in Cambridge has been drastically reduced. Most of the trade has moved online. But the Oxfam shops, somehow free from the killingly high levels of rent, were still worth visiting on those occasions when I could summon the strength to limp the half-mile into town. And always, in the Market Square, on Tuesdays and Thursdays, there was Hugh's bookstall, known to its devotees both literary and academic as one of the great bookstalls on earth.

As the laid-out stock is sold off during the day, the gaps are filled with yet more books from Hugh's seemingly inexhaustible supply of substantial hardbacks and paper-backs. Hugh doesn't say much, but those in the know tell me that he scores all this mouthwatering stuff at car boot sales. I suppose that the original owners of the books have died off, and their families have put the books back into the economy in the simplest way possible. As I was scheduled to die off myself, even if I did not precisely know when, it was madness to start making small piles of books on Hugh's stall that I wanted to take home. But the madness was divine. Even if I already had the book, he might have a handier edition; and often they were titles that I had once owned but lost along the way; and most often of all they were books that I had never owned before but now real-ized I ought to possess. Somewhere in there was an itching sense of duty. The childish urge to understand everything doesn't necessarily fade when the time approaches for you to do the most adult thing of all: vanish.

But these and similar philosophical principles will be treated from time to time throughout this volume. Finally you get to the age when a book's power to make you think becomes the first thing you notice about it. You can prac-tically sense that power when you pick the book up. The books I already had in the house presumably once generated the same sort of charge when I contemplated buying them. Now there they were, still in their thousands despite the recent winnowing. I roamed slowly among them: old purchases begging to be read again even as the new purchases came in at the rate of one plastic shopping bag full every week. Insanity, insanity. Or, as Johnson might have said, vanity, vanity.

Johnson, who often convicted himself of indolence, might possibly have approved my plan for the organization of this volume: there isn't one. It just sort of happened, and for several years I had been occupied with what might well have been my last readings before Yale kindly got the idea of asking me to compose a little book about whatever books I had been reading lately. Even after the request came, I went on reading in no particular order, mixing books of obvious seriousness with books of seeming triviality; as I always have, in the belief that culture is a matter not of credentials, but only of intensity, and sometimes you will find things out from fans and buffs that you won't from a tenured professor. Thus there were heavy books about Washington that taught me about American politics, but also featherweight books about Hollywood that taught me about American cultural imperialism: which is, after all, the branch of American global dominance that actually works, however much the rest of us might fret.

I also mixed books I had read before with books I ought not to have neglected. The second category, I found, tended to absorb the first; because if I had first read a book long enough ago, it seemed brand new when I came to it again. I suppose the big find, among those books truly new to me, was Olivia Manning's set of two trilogies; and the shock of pleasure that her writings delivered to me is recorded here with due prominence. But it was almost as much of a revelation, after more than fifty years, to rediscover Joseph Conrad. My *reconquista* of his works is spread throughout this book because that was the way it happened: I didn't revisit his major novels in a bunch, I tried to space them out, mainly because I was trying to stop. Time felt precious and I would have preferred to spend less of it with him, but he wouldn't let me go.

I might say the same of Ernest Hemingway; and at this point I really did have a dramatic order in mind while I wrote my text; I wanted him young and infinitely promising in my overture, and disintegrating in my finale. It seemed fair. Much of the damage that led to his terrible end he had inflicted on himself. And he seemed such a conspicuous example of how the gift of life, and the gift of talent, can be abused. Perhaps I was becoming Puritanical in my old age—dotards often do—but I disapproved of his recklessness, while attempting to register the undoubted fact that I would not have disapproved so much if he had not been such a mighty figure. He haunts this book, as Dr. Johnson does. But so do they all, the writers. Piled up, the books they wrote are not a necropolis. They are an arcadian pavilion with an infinite set of glittering, mirrored doorways to the unknown: which seems dark to us only because we will not be in it. We won't be taking our knowledge any further, but it brought us this far.

Hemingway in the Beginning

I LAST READ *The Sun Also Rises* long enough ago to have forgotten all but the odd detail. But the sharpness of the details I remembered—the chestnut trees of Paris, the running of the bulls in Pamplona—was a sufficient reminder that the book had always struck me as fresh and vivid, the perfect expression of a young writer getting into his proper stride. When I first read it I was a young writer myself, and scarcely into my stride at all. I remember that the book filled me with envy.

Reading it once again, and at the end of my own career, I am less envious—clearly Hemingway's own personality had always scared him into suicidal excess—but still enchanted by a prose style that gave us such a vivid semblance of simplicity. All too often he overdoes the repetitions in those dialogue passages where the speakers seem mainly intent on echoing each other's phrases. Worse, when they get drunk they start echoing themselves. But even with that irritating trick, he occasionally gets it so right that you laugh. Mike, the most consistently drunk of all the book's drunkards, is funny the second time that he says the old lady's bags fell on him: funny because he first said it only a few seconds before, and has either forgotten he did so or is under the impression that nobody understood him. It is just the way that young, inexperienced drinkers speak when they are plastered. I used to do it myself, fifty years ago.

In the book, scarcely anybody is old enough to have a past. They live in the present moment because they are young, and have to. So they pretend to be experienced. The central figure, Jake Barnes, has the author's past, except that Jake's past is not a lie. He might be the author's self-image, and not least because he lives in a state of permanent sexual frustration. Certainly Hemingway was always made nervous by women, although he was so attractive in his looks and energy that almost any woman he wanted would come to him like a mosquito to naked skin. Jake's impotence even in the presence of the beautiful English aristocratic wildcat Lady Brett Ashley no doubt dramatizes the author's wishes along with his troubles.

(In real life, on one of his first trips to Pamplona, Hemingway, with his first wife Hadley looking on, paid attention to Lady Duff Twysden and had a fistfight with his Jewish acquaintance Harold Loeb because Loeb had been successful with her.) But Jake is more physically damaged than mentally. The physical damage—its nature is never quite specified, although later on, in real life, Hemingway spoke of an amputation—has been acquired during the war when he was flying on the southern front. As a consequence, Jake and Brett are in a condition of lusting after each other without being able to do anything about it. The possibility of Jake's being able to do something less than complete for Brett but still significant is not canvassed, except in a single enigmatic passage in the book when the two of them seem to have attained just enough satisfaction to make them more frustrated than ever.

Today's reader might judge that to be a failure of the author's imagination. But there is no failure of the imagination in Hemingway's making Jake into a war pilot. It is exactly the kind of thing that Hemingway liked to imagine, in the same way he imagined himself to be a champion boxer, even on the day when Morley Callaghan knocked him down. (Callaghan's *That Summer in Paris* is another book I must read again.) Hemingway's war service, though earthbound, was dangerous enough to get him badly wounded, but he lied even about that, dramatizing, at every retelling, the action he had seen and even the wounds he had received. Later on, in *A Farewell to Arms*, Hemingway made the hero a warrior so damaged that the nymphlike nurse Catherine seems to be bringing him back from the dead. But already, in *The Sun Also Rises*, Hemingway had done better than that: or, if you like, worse. Creating the self-projected character of the noble and stoically frustrated Jake, Hemingway not only gave himself extra wounds. He gave himself wings.

He was not alone in painting a picture of himself as the ace flyer. William Faulkner was prone to doing the same, until he was caught at it. Faulkner could actually fly but he never flew in combat, although he allowed people to think he had. Hemingway was forever leaving room for you to think things. During World War II, in which he let it be known that he had personally liberated Paris, he did brave deeds that those responsible for the safety of the people around him devoutly wished that he would desist from doing. Most of the warlike tasks that he set for himself were more than half-crazy, but he always left room, in the telling, for his readers and listeners to believe that his follies had been a strategically important part of the Allied war effort. You would swear that he had arm-wrestled German submarines into submission.

In real life, many writers are liars. Perhaps, when starting off, they all are: no real story is ever as neat as the writer tells it. Politicians with a tendency to self-glorifying exaggeration usually get caught early and are advised by their handlers to cut it out, so that Hillary Clinton doesn't land more than once in Sarajevo "under sniper fire," and Joe Biden, who once expanded his every experience into an act of heroism, eventually learns to feign veracity. But writers have to advise themselves. In World War II the poet James Dickey was the navigator of a P-61 Black Widow night fighter operating in the Pacific. You would think that such a service record would be romantic enough, but he used to improve his past by hinting that he had been in on the missions to drop the atomic bombs on Japan. Unfortunately this self-serving legend—he was a man who needed more guilt than he deserved—got into his work, and even when he had a fact to convey he would pump it up so as to increase his own significance. Hemingway suffered from the same disease. Having noticed how the narrative charm of a seemingly objective style would put a gloss on reality automatically, he habitually trod on the accelerator instead of the brake. As a result, much of his later work was ruined. He overstated even the understatements. But with *The Sun Also Rises* he was still testing his power to enchant.

There is not much that is enchanting about his treatment of Robert Cohn, which must have sounded anti-Semitic even at the time, one would have thought. Nor is there anything enchanting about his repeated use of the word "nigger," but that's a problem for teachers and publishers, many of whom are African Americans but seem not to object much, as if—and this is true—Hemingway's little novel, which is really only an extended novella, was a thing of its time. Whether it is also a thing for eternity is debatable. Certainly it continues to count in my own eternity, but that will soon come to an end. In the short time I have left for reading, however, I am very glad to have found occasion for hearing once again how Jake and Brett adored each other in that strange, mannered, yet somehow sensual dialogue, as if a phrase could be a caress. The book is a metaphorical triumph, and all while having scarcely a single metaphor in it, or even a simile. In fact only once does Hemingway say that something is like something else. In Jake's mind, Brett's lovely figure has the curves of a racing yacht's hull. Our minds might tell us that a woman whose figure reminded us of a boat would be an awkward proposition, but our hearts are already captured.

Revisiting Conrad

AMONG THE DISADVANTAGES of COPD, which used
to be called emphysema, is a susceptibility to chest infec-
tions. Despite one's daily intake of antibiotics, different bac-
teria keep arriving from all directions, eager to squat. One
day I was checking in at the hospital for a routine clinic,
and my temperature was deemed to be too high for me to
go home. I spent ten days in the pulmonary ward, while
the fever turned into pneumonia. A flood of intravenous
antibiotics eventually got on top of it, but meanwhile the
problem of boredom loomed. I staved it off by rereading
Lord Jim, a copy of which, along with the usual epics about
swords and dragons, was on the library cart which a very
sweet and obviously fulfilled senior female volunteer was
wheeling around the wards. More than half a century ago
Lord Jim had been one of the set novels for my first-year
English class at Sydney University, and I remembered it as

a boring book. I suppose I had a plan to stave off one kind of boredom with another, as a kind of inoculation.

On the strength of this long-delayed second reading, the book struck me as no more exciting than it had once seemed, but a lot more interesting. I had long known Conrad to be a great writer: on the strength of *Under Western Eyes* alone, he would have to be ranked high among those English writers—well, Polish writers resident in England—who, dealing with eastern Europe, analyzed the struggle between the imbecility of autocracy and the imbecility of revolution. But on the strength of my earlier memories, I didn't see *Lord Jim* as part of that international historical picture. Now, reading a few pages at a time as I lay fitfully on a sweat-soaked sheet while my fever refused to break, I could see that I had been laughably wrong about Conrad's most famous book for the whole of my reading life. An international historical picture is exactly what it exemplifies.

But the picture, or viewpoint, is well guarded. In the first place, the story turns on a character study. Without Jim's weakness, there would be no story at all. At the beginning of the narrative, in his role as an officer in the mercantile marine, he jumps off a sinking ship that turns out not to have been sinking. He never gets over this: which raises the question, as we read on, of whether we ourselves could go on functioning if we were unable to forget our ignoble moments. At the end of the narrative, in his role as the de facto monarch of the magic kingdom of Patusan, he ruins the lives of his consort and his people by failing to accept that the pack of renegades who have penetrated their little Paradise might have evil in mind. The book's narrator, Marlow, puts Jim's failings down to his romantic personality: his later life is "an expiation for his craving after more glamour than he could carry." We, the enthralled readers, are at liberty to deduce that European politics have infected the whole world, even the parts of it that are not yet known: the renegades would not have come if Jim had not made Patusan just and prosperous.

Unfortunately, for us enthralled readers, the story is not quite enthralling enough. Marlow is telling it, and Marlow is a bore. He is Conrad's sole tedious creation, because ordinarily Conrad can see the point of anything completely and at once, whereas Marlow feeds you information only a few drops at a time. Perhaps because I had an I.V. plugged into my arm, I couldn't help thinking of the last chick in the clutch wasting away from getting not quite enough food.

Marlow was a useful device if you thought the book's revelations needed delaying, but his terrific ability for beating around the bush was bound to register as a tease play. I finished reading the book though, full of admiration for both Conrad and myself: him for his moral scope, me for my endurance. Perhaps to induce self-esteem in the reader had been one of the author's aims. There are those who believe that Wagner made *Siegfried* so wearisome because he wanted the audience to admire themselves.

Anyway, when I got home I reached for my old copy of *Nostromo*. Long ago, just after I had read *Lord Jim*, I had read *Nostromo* too, and been deeply impressed. There was, after all, no Marlow in it: the narrator's voice came through unfiltered by an intervening cloth of tedium. But now, reading again, I wondered how I had coped with an English novel's plentiful supply of Spanish words. How could I have been impressed, instead of puzzled and put off? Eventually, after more than twenty years of not being able to read any Spanish at all, I acquired enough to assess what I had been missing. Now, finally, when Conrad referred to the *capataz de cargadores,* I could tell for sure that he meant Nostromo. Also, I had learned a great deal more about politics. Years of reading in modern history had equipped me to understand retroactively the lethality of the historic events that Conrad seemed to know about in advance, so sensitive was he to the political forces that were already reshaping the world during his own lifetime. In my own lifetime, most of the reshaping actually got done, with a death count of many millions. It's clear now that Conrad had guessed what might happen. But when I first read *Nostromo* I was too young to have much of a clue even about what had already happened. So what had impressed me?

Undoubtedly it was the story, in the Hollywood sense, which means the scenario. The events are thrilling. Don Carlos Gould and his excellent wife build Sulaco into a kingdom with all the enchantment of Jim's Patusan, but Sulaco, on the page, is more actual in its workings. You can hear the ring of picks and hammers as the silver is torn from the mine. It's like *Das Rheingold* with the lights turned on. All the practical details of a foreign-owned capitalist enterprise are laid out, not just hinted at. Every supporting role is blazingly alive. They are all there: the corrupt dictator, the predecessor of so many Trujillos and

Batistas; the local wiseacre who knows everything and understands nothing; and the beautiful girl with the book of poetry in her hand, all set, by her mere existence, to lead the previously feckless young intellectual editor fatally away from his usual protective cynicism. Idealism gets him killed. Above all, there is Nostromo (did I know, first time around, that his Italianized nickname meant "our man"?), who has built such a reputation for competence and integrity that the gringo ruling class revere him, not for a moment suspecting that the man they trusted never to steal an ounce of silver would eventually steal a ton of it. He didn't suspect it either: but when the moment came, he overruled any loyalty except to himself.

And those themes are only the beginning of what is in *Nostromo,* which I can now see as one of the greatest books I have ever read. But I thought the same when I had read almost no serious books at all. Somewhere in that paradox lies the secret of a magic novel, and the secret of why the later novels of Henry James have never held me in a spell: in the opening chapters, their subtleties of style catch the attention of the experienced reader in me, but the inexperienced reader in me finds too little to draw him forward. If only Henry James had been to sea. But Edith Wharton's account of how he rambled on incomprehensibly when he got out of the car to ask directions tells us that any order he delivered on the bridge would have been so elaborately expressed that the ship would have hit something on the first day of the voyage.

Novels in Sequence

I HAVE JUST STARTED to read Edward St. Aubyn's latest novel, *Lost for Words*, and I can already see that I will have to double back and get on terms with his Patrick Melrose sequence. James Wood and Will Self both have a right to say that St. Aubyn is witty, even if the rest of us find him only witty-ish. Most writers who are credited with wit have not a trace of it, but St. Aubyn really can pack the meaning tight enough for it to crackle, and he can do so often enough to make you impatient when he doesn't. St. Aubyn's imaginary publishing house called Page and Turner is memorable straight away, whereas Anthony Powell put half a novel into explaining the nickname of Books-do-furnish-a-room Bagshaw and still couldn't make it interesting. Kenneth Widmerpool, the figure of ambitious mediocrity whose relentless climb to power links all the novels of Powell's great sequence, is a joke for the ages, but Bagshaw, because he is a joke and nothing else, is scarcely a joke at all.

Though St. Aubyn actually has the British upper-class background that Evelyn Waugh would have liked for himself, it is interesting that the Melrose books are such a hit in the United States. Thus a form not native to America is now being imported. In America, it is as if novels have to be individuals, like people. I suppose James T. Farrell's Studs Lonigan books and Philip Roth's Zuckerman books are among the exceptions; and certainly John Updike found it congenial to stretch the interior lives of Rabbit Angstrom and Henry Bech over several volumes; but generally the *roman fleuve* is not an American native growth. In Britain, specifically in England, it is as natural as a row of willows.

But the English novel sequences still looked like a big ask, until I found myself reading Evelyn Waugh's *Sword of Honour* trilogy all over again. It had been a while since I had read its constituent books, with the usual feeling one has, when reading Waugh, that the prose is designed to go down like a glass of water. Now, reading them again, I was more carried away than ever. I could quite see that Apthorpe and his thunder box were not as funny as they were cracked up to be—people who find Waugh unamusing usually harp on that point, as if they had something against outside lavatories—but the narrative drive was irresistible, even if the whole thing was plainly a wish fulfillment. Waugh pictured himself as the effective military officer that he in fact was not, just as he would always behave, even before he had the money, like the landed gentleman that he in fact was not. (Waugh seems to be admitting, through the persona of Crouchback, that he might have been more effective still, but his accursed gentlemanliness got in the way. The truth is more likely to have been that Waugh's troops didn't dislike him for his superior manners, they loathed him for his rudeness.) Some of the individual novels—even the often despised *Brideshead Revisited*—leave *Sword of Honour* looking like a grab bag. *Scoop* and *A Handful of Dust* are miracles of neat concentration, and *Decline and Fall,* for comic boldness, is beyond praise: the protracted demise of little Lord Tangent ought not to be hilarious, but it is. Nevertheless, *Sword of Honour* has the broadness of concept that makes Waugh's other novels look as if pennies are being pinched. In them, he is spending judiciously from his hoard, whereas in *Sword of Honour* he is betting the whole bundle.

But this was merely rereading, whereas there were novel sequences I had not read at all; or, sometimes, read only in part; or, shamefully, knew only from the television adaptation. Under that last classification came the two sequences by Olivia Manning, the Balkan trilogy and the Levant trilogy. Back in 1987 there was a BBC television adaptation, called *Fortunes of War*, that squeezed the two sequences into a single series, and was so good I somehow decided afterward that I knew all I needed to know about the books it was based on. The portrayal of the two leading characters was perfect: Kenneth Branagh as Guy Pringle looked just the type to be so enslaved by his haversack full of books that he would always get the actual world wrong, and Emma Thompson as his wife, Harriet, embodied the unused qualities of sensitivity and practicality that continually underlined just why she shouldn't be married to Guy. But married they were: he a case of useless intelligence, she a case of wasted love. How could the actual novels be as vivid as that?

Well, lately I have read them all, and they are as vivid as that: even more so. Beyond the scope of any camera, the writing gives us the rich depth of the exotic settings, always more detailed when seen from Harriet's viewpoint than from Guy's. And minor characters that were already sharply defined on screen—the extravagant sponge Yakimov, the appalling Professor Pinkrose—are now made fascinating, instead of merely entertaining, as Manning's style delves into their interior lives. Most remarkable of all her qualities as a writer, however, is her historical grasp. You could say that there had always been English female writers equipped to evoke a world beyond the English Channel. In the nineteenth century, Mrs. Oliphant's book on Florence was only one of many such books written by women; and early in the next century Gertrude Bell wrote substantial volumes about Middle Eastern states that she actually helped to build. (Iraq was partly her creation.) In 1941, Rebecca West published *Black Lamb and Grey Falcon,* a densely written two-volume magnum opus about Yugoslavia. But these were all factual works. Few women, and indeed few men, had written fiction that took in the sweep of modern history. Olivia Manning did it. This, we feel, is how it must have been: the troubled territories with which we are now doomed to cope are all there in her clear river of prose. Recognizing the world that Harriet puts together in her mind as she persuades the hopelessly optimistic Guy, in one collapsing country after another, to get out while there is still time, the reader can draw solace. Doom feels a bit better.

How great was she? Deirdre David, who has written a rewarding book about Manning's life, treats her as a giant. Having read the two trilogies, and then Deirdre David's book as a follow-up, I feel bound to say that Ms. David is right—feel bound, that is, because Manning is still not getting the attention she deserves. She deserves something better than mere fame. She needs her reputation raised to the level of unarguable fact. (Rachel Cooke, in her excellent book *Her Brilliant Career*, which assesses the significance of ten women who came to prominence in the 1950s, gives Manning a chapter that sets the necessary tone.)

Manning is a magisterial writer, the master spirit of her chosen genre. A quick way of conveying her stature as a sequential novelist would be to say that she is up there with Ford Madox Ford in his Tietjens tetralogy; with Paul Scott and his *Raj Quartet;* with Waugh's *Sword of Honour* trilogy; and with the twelve volumes of Anthony Powell's *A Dance to the Music of Time*. She is more than up there with Lawrence Durrell's *Alexandria Quartet,* she is far above it: fifty years ago, Durrell's epic was famous, but really it should have been judged as a mass of purple patches even then, and now it reads like a whole platter of overripe fruit.

But a better way to raise the stakes would be to bring in the name of Proust. Often invoked when discussing Anthony Powell, Proust seems to me just as relevant to Manning; although I can see that I might think this merely because I am currently under the spell of her style, and need to read Powell again. In general, however, we can surely say that Manning took the same opportunity as Proust did in using the expanse of her creation to lay out an oncoming historical tendency. In Proust's case it was his perception of how the high society he loved was being riddled with an anti-Semitism that was bound to have long-term consequences, and in Manning's case it was a perception of how Europe's *mission civilisatrice* in the countries to the south and east was bound to fail, partly because Europe itself was less civilized than it liked to believe. Both writers enriched the future by fully illuminating the recent past. You could just about say Paul Scott did the same: in the *Raj Quartet*, British India can be seen to crumble.

The driving force of both Waugh and Powell, however, was their vision of how the traditional English social order was falling apart. In their one-off novels they might have had an international scope, but when it came to writing a big masterpiece, both of them were more interested in a changing homeland than in a changing world. As for Ford Madox Ford—who can be seen as the modern instigator of the sequential form, if you don't want to count Trollope and his Paliser novels—the effect of the *Parade's End* novels is to take World War I personally. His standalone novel *The Good Soldier* is a better book because less self-serving. Tietjens, as a character, is the merest wish fulfillment, the self-indulgence of a mendacious, chaotic, casually womanizing author who would like to project himself as a pillar of integrity and self-sacrifice, the honest master of his feelings. (In this respect, Tietjens is a prototype for Waugh's Guy Crouchback, the author's daydream about what he would like to have been, instead of a portrayal of what he was.) There is nothing self-serving about Manning's Harriet. She, not Guy, is the hero of the two sequences; and the two sequences, taken together, outstrip anything else on our list for the sense they convey that the author sees the world as it is, and as it is bound to become, tragic experience having planted itself so deeply in the texture of time. Her great creation leads from then to now, and makes now more bearable.

Patrick O'Brian and His Salty Hero

MY ELDER DAUGHTER should take some of the credit, or blame, for getting me to start reading again as if there might be a tomorrow, when I was ready to settle down on my deathbed and read nothing but the Bible. She had all of Patrick O'Brian's Jack Aubrey novels in her house and urged me to try the first one, *Master and Commander,* with a promise that it was even better than the movie. She was like a drug dealer handing out a free sample. Within a few days I was back for the next one, *Post Captain,* and in the course of remarkably little time—the excitement of reading stopped me reminding myself that it was time I didn't really have—I had read all twenty volumes. I found that my mental image of Jack Aubrey's physical appearance never shifted. To my mind, he looked exactly like Russell Crowe. But Aubrey's abilities and ambitions fascinated me, to the point where I started wondering whether

I might have been a better man if I had gone to sea. Very early in my life, while I was still an adolescent who read voraciously but not seriously, Kipling's *Captain's Courageous* had had the same effect: an effect only reinforced by C. S. Forester's Hornblower books. But now here I was, at the other end of life, and once again I was hero-worshiping an example of leadership, discipline, and carelessness of danger. My admiration for Aubrey would have been absurd if I had not detected that O'Brian was daydreaming on his own account. He was escaping from the pettiness of today into the supposed high values of yesterday. His hero was a time traveler.

Nevertheless, Aubrey brooks no belittling, even as a musician. He plays his violin on the night before battle, but the author assures us that his musicianship is enthusiastically workmanlike at best. He is good with the strings but better at climbing ropes. O'Brian does not do the usual thing and give his hero a whole range of talents at the genius level. When Conan Doyle invented Sherlock Holmes, he showered the sleuth with extra gifts: the infallible detective was an expert in many fields, seemingly without ever having studied them. This best-selling tendency to make the man of action a *uomo universale* went all the way down to James Bond, who, were he not a spy, could be a linguist. O'Brian doesn't suggest that Aubrey, were he not the captain of a frigate, could be Isaac Stern. O'Brian's restraint in this matter was an important act of self-discipline, because the temptation is always there to turn the superior character into superman. John le Carré had something going with George Smiley but should have abandoned him earlier. When, in *The Honourable School-boy*, Smiley revealed a hitherto unsuspected knowledge of ancient Chinese naval architecture, it was high time to toss him over the Reichenbach Falls. It might not have worked, however. It didn't work with Sherlock, who refused to be eliminated, and came back because the public couldn't get enough of him.

The public never got enough of Jack Aubrey, but eventually O'Brian was caught by death after having made a start on the twenty-first volume, so a twenty-volume series is all we have. My own theory is that Aubrey could have ended up as First Sea Lord and still have been interesting, but that there was an automatic terminus to our interest in Aubrey's buddy, Stephen Maturin. Increasingly as the sequence goes on, Stephen's chief function is to fall through hatches or off the back of the ship. A greatly talented physician, everyone's dream of a ship's doctor, he is still a stooge: like Peter Sellers as Inspector Clouseau, Stephen can't stay coordinated for five minutes, except when he unexpectedly turns out to be a crack shot. But even then, he can't shoot as accurately as he can fall headfirst down a companionway. It makes you wonder about what kind of surgery he is doing down there belowdecks when the ship is reeling under the impact of massed French cannon.

O'Brian doesn't really know what to do with an interesting female character. The only woman on a par with the leading men gets killed off in a coach accident. No, these are boys' books, and the lesser for it. I try to remember that most of the fans of O'Brian that I have met are women, but I suspect that they want a holiday from feminism, just as his male fans want a holiday from inertia. (I should leave room at this point for the possibility that some of the female Aubrey experts in my vicinity see no contradiction between feminism and their allegiance to the age of sail, and quite fancy the picture of themselves dressed as commodores with epaulettes.) But if the Jack Aubrey books are merely entertaining, they are that at a high level. Part of the charm of O'Brian's magnificently decorated sequence—it makes me think of the bowsprit on HMS *Victory*—is the continuous and lavish deployment of seafaring terminology. Scuttle the larboard strakes! Every sheet and cleat is named. It doesn't matter much if you don't know what he is talking about. Aubrey has to tell Stephen what a "cunt splice" is. I didn't know either, and still don't; and even Google was too shy to speak on the subject; but I was ensnared by yet another example of the salt-sprayed vocabulary. It really does help to learn the names of all the sails; but then, the same thing helped when one was reading the Hornblower books, all those years ago.

Today, I should perhaps read Forester again. Here again, the screen images are so powerful they almost convince you that you don't need to open the books. In the movies, Gregory Peck was an ideal Hornblower. (Imagine Burt Lancaster in the same role: with bared teeth and somersaulting through the spars, he would have been the Crimson Pirate in a different hat.) And I have several times each seen all the Hornblower stories well done on television. Ioan Gruffudd is excellent casting in the title role, because he looks pensive; just as Russell Crowe is well cast as Aubrey, because Crowe, while always looking to be on the verge of converting himself into Oliver Hardy, is a thick-necked ball of energy; and O'Brian, though he gives Aubrey a fine practical mind, has made him as much of a man of action as Forester made Hornblower a sensitive thinker. On being drawn into the comparison, however, I have to say that the Aubrey fans who surround me—there are several people within a hundred yards of my house who own the complete set of novels, neatly lined up—enrage me when they praise Aubrey at Hornblower's expense. Yes, I must read the Hornblower books again soon, if only to confirm my memories of them as a brilliant sequential creation. According to my recollection, Hornblower is at least as good a portrait as Aubrey of a man rising through the navy because his talent is seen to be more forceful than the system of seniority that would like to keep him down. And isn't Forester's technical vocabulary just as detailed and poetic, even though there are no cunt splices in it? Other times, other customs.

War Leader

IN THE COURSE OF a lifetime's intake of books about the leading figures in World War II—having been born only a month after it started, I have always felt that those years were the beginning of my schooling—I somehow didn't get round to reading General Sir David Fraser's biography *Alanbrooke*. I should have. It is not only well written, it is well judged. That second quality is important because the hidden hero is Churchill, and anyone writing about the war from the British angle must have the critical scope to see that although Britain would not have survived without him, the war would have been lost if he had been left to himself. Churchill needed a lot of handling, or he would always be off on some wasteful scheme; and his handlers were a special breed. They had to respect his spirit, but if they couldn't rein in his wilder plans, they were useless. I probably won't feel the need to read Lord

Ismay's memoirs again, but I can remember that I was full of admiration for the bravery, common sense, and efficiency of Churchill's chief military assistant, a normal man who learned how to serve a genius.

Alanbrooke, by Fraser's account, was of the same stamp. He started from a privileged background, and was lucky, in the First World War, to be an officer of artillery rather than of infantry: the death rate was much lower. In India there was always polo, but Alan Brooke (as he then was: he didn't become Lord Alanbrooke until after World War II) was so well connected that he could still pursue his shooting and riding when he got back to England, where those hallowed aristocratic activities were a lot harder on the pocket. Capable as well as clubbable, he went steadily upward into the higher ranks until finally he was C.I.G.S. (Chief of the Imperial General Staff), where he was just in time to help save his nation from the potentially deadly combination of Nazi barbarity and Churchillian enthusiasm. A clear, logical speaker—with the sole drawback that he talked too quickly, especially for the Americans— he would fearlessly read Churchill the riot act. For a subordinate to fearlessly contradict his boss, it helps if he is not afraid to lose his job: the chief advantage of having been brought up well-off and well placed. Even the Americans, normally suspicious of toffs, were impressed with Brooke, although they didn't like the sound of that word "Imperial" in the title of his job. But for the nonce, the British and the Americans were not at loggerheads about their plans for the future: they were brothers in arms in the present, and if D-Day can be counted as a triumph for one man, that one man was Brooke. He made sure that the potentially explosive combination of Eisenhower and Montgomery remained potential.

One of the secrets of his plainspoken dominance—in the office, he always expressed himself in the minimum of words—was that he was secretly a master of improvised talk, and at the dinner table he would let the secret out, charming everyone present. Since he had spoken French before he spoke English, he could disarm even the Free French leaders, who were always apprehensive that they might be patronized. A star talker doesn't necessarily have to be a mimic, but a surprising number of them are. (I have no gift for mimicry myself, but wish I did.) Reputedly, Brooke's mimicry was perfect. I wish I could have heard it.

In my time I have been lucky enough to share a table with Peter Bogdanovich, whose mimicry is so accurate that he doesn't need to be funny: he is, but you would be riveted even if he weren't. Kingsley Amis was a great mimic. Having heard him many times in his later life, I can well believe Philip Larkin's story of how his future friend, when they first met in Oxford, staged a gunfight with what sounded like real guns. Kingsley's son Martin can do it too, although I notice that he has been wise enough never to do it for journalists, who would manufacture reams of copy with such evidence of his multiple identity, etc. I once spent two weeks filming a television special about Mel Gibson, and he would not be drawn into revealing even a hint of his ability to "do" the voice of any male film star since sound came in. This knack was famous among his friends, but in front of my camera he wasn't going to give away the magic. He was right, of course. Half the secret of public life is not to blur the image. Gibson wanted to be thought of as an actor, not as a vaudeville turn; just as Alanbrooke wanted to be thought of as a soldier. Short of manpower and money, always building the wrong tanks, Britain in World War II was lucky in its senior officers; the traditional military caste, for the last but most crucial time in the nation's history, came through with the goods. It should be added, however, that by the time of the Falklands War the armed forces were being ably led by "the boys from the state schools." It had been Churchill's phrase, coined during the Battle of Britain: he had foreseen the future, and guessed that it would work.

But during the war, the British forces, with the possible exception of the RAF, had toffs at the top. In view of that fact, it remains remarkable that the Americans so smoothly accepted the alliance. A lot of the bonding happened between Churchill and Roosevelt, but the next level down was the crucial one, and on that level it was a sheer fluke that the very American George Marshall and the very British Alan Brooke could have talked strategy together without grasping each other by the throat. Helping them reach harmony was the stroke of luck by which the Americans themselves thought the Germany First strategy was the way to proceed, so the British didn't have to sell them the idea: they were already working on it. But the whole business of a joint command that operated on both sides of the Atlantic simultaneously is an inspiration to read about, because it shows what democratic nations can do when the chips are down. Lately I have been reading what I would guess to be the best book on the subject (it's a theme that nearly all the military historians have taken a crack at): *Masters and Commanders,* by Andrew Roberts. Of the book's many virtues, the most important is that the author knows how to bring the four main characters alive: Churchill, Roosevelt, Marshall, and Brooke are all there, at least three of them acting more strangely than you might have imagined. But if Hitler and Tojo could have put together a team like that, the world would have been lost.

Sebald and the Battle in the Air

AN ADMIRER OF W. G. Sebald, I know my way around the often intricate paths of all his major books up to and including the magnificent *Austerlitz*, but I had never read his little book about the Allied air war against Nazi Germany. I was put off by the reviews, which, even when they praised the book, did too good a job of outlining the essential fatuity of its thesis. According to Sebald, German literature after the war had never faced up to the subject of the bombing raids. That much was perhaps true, but Sebald had gone on to claim that the subject was therefore a lacuna in the German national consciousness. Since I have always been convinced that a national consciousness is formed by secondary writing rather than by serious writing, I put off reading the book: why spend time reading even a great writer when he was trying to make bricks without straw?

But finally the book came and got me, in the form of a thin Fischer paperback on Hugh's bookstall in the Cambridge marketplace. Already before I had paid for it and taken it away, I was deep into *Luftkrieg und Literatur*. The prose, being Sebald's, was exquisite. His manner of squeezing historical significance from objects and landscapes—a manner which has by now filtered down to such best sellers as Edmund de Waal's *The Hare with Amber Eyes*—was as seductive as ever. But the basic idea was, for him, uniquely nonprofound. He hadn't even considered that the generation of young male readers in postwar Germany might have learned, while growing up, all about the air war from quite another source than serious literature. He grew up in Germany himself—he didn't move to Britain until 1965—but he seems not to have read much of the unserious literature that his fellow Germans were reading in their childhood and adolescence: unserious literature in which the air raids were a prominent theme. In the kind of war-story magazines that seldom end up in libraries, there were sensationally illustrated articles about German night-fighter pilots flying into action against the RAF four-engine bombers that had come to devastate the German cities. The magazines were pulp, but the story they were telling was true, and young German boys—probably not the girls, but for anyone except the Russians the air war was a man's world—did their first reading about the war the same way I did. Out there in Australia, I read *Flames in the Sky*, by Pierre Clostermann, and dozens of other books like it. In Germany, the youngsters read about such highly decorated night flyers as Major Heinz Wolfgang Schnaufer, who shot down a scarcely believable 121 RAF bombers. Books with cheap titles like *Luftwaffe at War* showed young war buffs of the English-speaking world what the air war over Europe had been like. Except, apparently, for Sebald, Germans of my age saw books just like them: hundreds of photographs, but with the captions in their language instead of ours. Sometimes the captions were approximately informed junk, but in many cases they were expertly done. Put all that pulp and glossy publishing together and it added up to an information system: a system that helped prepare a young intelligence to make properly considered judgments later on. It was information that Sebald could have made something of, if he had seen enough of it. But it seems likely that he was shut off from informatively trivial publications by his exclusive concern with serious publications, and in this one area he ended up running thin on facts. In *Austerlitz* he can write a sublime cantata dedicated to Liverpool Street Station because he turned himself back into a wide-eyed young observer before he sat down to write. About that subject, to achieve his adult prose, he did the childish thing, and became a fan. About the air war, he didn't have the same deep background.

On the market stall I picked up one of those elementary-looking, large-format illustrated war books in which it is a moot point whether the chapters are long captions or the captions are short chapters. Purporting to be an account of the Luftwaffe from 1933 to 1945, this one was called *Hitler's Eagles:* an unpromising title. There was even less promise in the author's name: Chris McNab. He sounded as if he might also have written picture books about motorcycles. But after only a quick skip-through, *Hitler's Eagles* stood revealed as the work of an expert, so I broke my own embargo—no more picture books about anything—and took it home.

Most of the pictures of German planes and pilots I had seen before in the Nazi magazine *Signal,* from which a file of extracts is still on my shelves even after the most recent culling of my books. (My great source for that kind of stuff, incidentally, used to be one of the bookstalls under the arches at Friedrichstrasse railway station. I would go there whenever I was in Berlin, but since I got sick I have not been back.) There were only so many photographs of, say, Werner Hartmann, the Luftwaffe ace of aces who shot down an astonishing 352 enemy aircraft, most of them on the Eastern Front. By now all the photographs of him and his fellow aces have shown up somewhere; and likewise there will probably be no more previously unseen images of the Me262 jet fighters as they taxied out to use up the last few drops of Nazi Germany's fuel. But the text is full of observation, judgment, and accurate detail, and those things are always new.

An excellent chapter on the night fighters tells us that in the last phase of the war they were pressed into service against the American bombers in daylight, with shocking losses. Weighed down by their radar equipment and aerials, they were easy meat for the American long-range day fighters. McNab has read the German sources and knows that in the group of Pathfinders assigned to mark the target for an RAF night raid, the leading plane was nicknamed the *Zeremonienmeister* (master of ceremonies). This is the kind of detail which tends to run thin in the more serious histories: their authors just aren't thrilled enough by the machinery. You could call it Small Boys' Knowledge: in my generation, the generation which is now growing old and getting ready to die, there were always small boys who could name the planes in the images. But for quite a while now a new generation has been in charge of communications, and they either don't know or don't care. It's an inevitable declension: in my own time as a writer-narrator of television documentaries, few of the young researchers could understand why I got so exercised about footage of the wrong plane dropping bombs on the wrong place. Just as long as it was a plane and it was dropping bombs on something, they protested, it fitted my narrative. (They were equally puzzled when I flipped my lid at the spectacle of the wrong tanks going the wrong way in the wrong war.) And I suppose that, time having elapsed, they were bound not to see the point, just as I don't care much whether the Roman chariots racing on screen are of the wrong type, as long as they don't have exhaust pipes. (Strangely, Hollywood, which is famous for playing fast and loose with historical detail, was always fanatical about the authenticity of the hardware. The production design departments were hotbeds of pertinent knowledge; it was the dialogue that was anachronistic, and no studio mogul ever cared as long as the scene played well.) Apropos, the paper cover of Sebald's little book about how the Germans have never known enough about the air war against the Reich carries a photograph that suggests he never knew enough about it either. If he okayed the cover picture, he okayed the wrong thing. The twin-engine planes flying low over the burned-out Reichstag are not American or British bombers. Almost certainly they are Russian, finally showing up over Berlin in the very last hours of the war. (Anyone familiar with that particular image knows that if you pull back a bit, there is a Russian tank in the foreground.) The Russian air force, mainly a tactical weapon to be used over the battleground, wasn't really part of the Allied air attack on Germany that Sebald talks about. But the publisher's art department was full of young people who didn't know the difference between one aircraft and another, and I suppose we should be glad that the day will come when hardly anybody knows, except the kind of machine buff who could equally be compiling a picture book about the history of customized motorcycles in California.

Phantom Flying Saucer

IF A BOOK CONTAINS hard facts about World War II, I find it hard to toss it aside even when the author inadvertently makes clear that he has fallen for a journalistic myth. I'm too scared of missing something vital. In *Last Days of the Reich*, James Lucas tells the awful story, not often enough told, of the atrocities that went on after the war was over. In some of the countries which had come under the control of the Soviet Union, or else of the Communist partisans, the locals strove to show any German civilians they could catch that the behavior of the Wehrmacht and the SS in Russia could have its counterpart in central Europe now that the tables had been turned. Hounded to death by the thousands, the victims were innocent civilians; but the victors were working on the principle that nobody was an innocent civilian. James Lucas, who died in 2002, was the author of a whole row of secondary books about various aspects of the war: the kind of book that is useful but not really essential. His *Last Days of the Reich*, however, would come close to being essential if it did not demonstrate at one point that the author can't tell a fact from a myth. He reports that the German aircraft industry, in its last phase before it ran out of petrol, developed a flying saucer that flew at eighteen hundred miles an hour. Connoisseurs of sensationalist rubbish will have met this German flying saucer before. In *Brighter than a Thousand Suns*, Robert Jungk's international best seller of 1970, the German flying saucer put in an appearance as if Jungk knew all about it. Excited journalists had to be told by aviation experts that if the Germans had developed a high-speed saucer, then it would have been copied straight after the war by either the United States or the Soviet Union, or perhaps by both. Already in contention for military supremacy, the two victorious superpowers had taken all the German aircraft industry's experts and documents home. Besides, there could have been no such leap forward by an aircraft unless there was an engine to propel it. There was no such engine, nor any prospect of one. And so on: for once, the facts were so overwhelming that they even managed to kill a media myth, which is usually hard to do.

World War II was, and remains, a potent inspiration to fantasy. There were people who were actually in the war who came away believing things that they should have known to be impossible. Gore Vidal would have been among the U.S. service personnel who invaded Japan if the atomic bombs had not been dropped. Yet he believed until the day he died that President Roosevelt tricked Japan into the war. There were plenty of ultra-right-wing Japanese madmen who were glad to have his support for their views; but really there was less than nothing in the idea. As the scientists say, the theory was so bad that it wasn't even wrong.

Under Western Eyes

SUDDENLY I AM reading *Under Western Eyes* again. I had vowed not to reread the whole of Conrad, but after a lifetime spent in the world that he presaged, I realize that I am at last ready for him. Much of the presaging is encapsulated in *Under Western Eyes*.

In Switzerland before World War I, before the tragedy in Europe, and before the chaos of the Russian Revolution, the Russians who gather in Geneva to enjoy democratic freedom—their part of the city is nicknamed Le Petit Russie—are already carrying within them all the varieties of doom that will soon engulf their land of origin. The book gives us a preview of the terrors to come. Some of the characters, indeed, are outright terrorists; but the majority of the radicals on view have as yet seen little of the life of action, although they talk a lot of theory. And some of the characters will be victims one day, if they do not have the sense to stay away: they are members of the aristocracy and the bourgeoisie, and they tend to think that tsarist despotism is the worst thing that their homeland has to offer.

They are in fact, idealists: and idealism is a cast of mind that Conrad questions even more than he questions radicalism. The logical end of radicalism, in his view, is terrorism; but idealism is the mental aberration that allows terror to be brought about. Conrad's originality was to see that a new tyranny could be generated by people who thought that their rebellion against the old tyranny was rational. Thus his writings seem prescient about what was to happen in the Soviet Union. He didn't predict the Nazi tyranny because he had underestimated the power of the irrational to organize itself into a state. But then, nobody predicted that except its perpetrators; and anyway, mere prediction was not his business. His business was the psychological analysis made possible by an acute historical awareness. *Under Western Eyes* is valuable not because it came true but because it rang true even at the time, only now we can better hear the deep, sad note.

The book's antihero, Razumov, is Lord Jim all over again; although this time Jim has started off, in Petersburg, by getting someone killed, and now, in Switzerland, must face the dilemma of having fallen in love with the victim's sister, and being unable to tell her. She is a wonderful character, Natalia Hardin: operatically attractive yet sensitive to the point of being saintly. But she is an idealist. In the end she will go home to Russia, in order to do good. Conrad published the book in 1911, when the Revolution was still six years in the future: but he got all the contending forces into the story, and the future along with them: the perfect girl, a living synthesis of everything praiseworthy and desirable, is heading for an appointment in which her superior qualities will not be forgiven. Or so we think; so history makes us think, after Conrad and the very few writers of comparable greatness have shown us what history is. The book takes a little too long to end, but a reader today should not miss the author's note at the start. Describing the unplumbably evil torturer Necator, Conrad calls him "the perfect flower of the terroristic wilderness. What troubled me most in dealing with him was not his monstrosity but his banality." Later in the century, Hannah Arendt was to say almost the same thing about Adolf Eichmann. She made the mistake, however, of finding his banality more remarkable than his monstrosity. Conrad, had he lived that long, could have told her that the two things, though one of them might be the more difficult to describe, are both as fundamental to evil as hydrogen and oxygen are to water.

Anthony Powell, Time Lord

HAVING REREAD SOME of the twentieth-century English novel sequences, and having read Olivia Manning's two trilogies for the first, belated time and realized she was great, I was determined not to go back to Anthony Powell. I thought my opinion of *A Dance to the Music of Time* was fully formed and would need no alteration: the sequence, as I recalled, was absorbing almost throughout, but at the end it went off precipitately. And even early on, there was evidence that its signature technique of teasing out the subtleties of any social incident, however minor, was too often strained beyond the limit. For half the time, the incident would be worth the trouble he took to reflect upon it; but for the other half, the effect of prosing away for pages about the repercussions of some minor accident suffered by an even more minor character would be, if not perhaps a fuss about nothing, certainly an endless palaver about not enough. And the clear prose could get into a tangle over the course of a long sentence.

All this I thought I remembered well. Also I had lost somewhere, in a move from a previous house, my precious set of the twelve Penguin volumes with the cover drawings by Osbert Lancaster. In yet another house there sat an American four-volume hardback edition, but the Americans had, in their usual way, overdone the reverence, so that any of the four compilations was too bulky to take on a train, thus defeating one of the chief pleasures that Powell offers: to read, while traveling in a second-class carriage, about the kind of people who used to travel in first.

No, let Powell rest in the memory. But what happened next you can guess. For once I got to Hugh's bookstall early enough in the day to catch the first wave of books, and there among them, spine upward, were all twelve volumes of the Mandarin paperback edition of *The Music of Time* with the cover illustrations by Mark Boxer. Like all Boxer's friends I had missed him fiercely since his premature death. He had once illustrated several books of mine, with results I had better not praise, although I was very proud to have his collaboration; and for Powell he was ideal, since Powell was minutely versed in social notation, and Boxer had the same fine focus. In fact Boxer was fully as good as Osbert Lancaster, who had been Powell's close friend. (It was because the Penguin editors stupidly wanted to ditch Lancaster's cover illustrations for the next reprint that Powell had left Penguin, his sardonic upper lip curled in contempt.) Mark Boxer, having been born much later than Powell and Lancaster, did not share their store of prewar experience, but he knew how to imagine himself into the past, and I think anyone who loves the books can see that those Mandarin volumes look as good as they read well.

And they do read well, as I soon found out all over again; because when I got them home I started reading them one after the other. In the last years of his life I knew Powell well enough to be sure he would have approved of how I relished the actual physical experience of consuming his little books like plates of sweets and grapes as I sat on my garden terrace while the heat gradually went out of a long summer. As an Australian I never love England more than at such times: they remind me of home, but are so much less fierce that they also remind me I was right to come away. Powell inspires you to reflections like that. He's good on the significance of the passing moment, his key message being that it doesn't really pass, but is incorporated into the texture of your reflections just as thoroughly as the ecstasies and disasters, and perhaps even more so.

This latest rereading of Powell soon put my admiration for the newfound Olivia Manning in its right context. She is great, but Powell's scope is even greater. The way the characters go on meeting one another through time, and the way that those who endure are always exchanging information about those who will not, is just like life. He is sometimes accused of overdoing the device of coincidence, but life does too; and in that regard he has given us, in what might be called the Powell Moment, a measure of consolation for those unsettling occasions when coincidence seems to threaten us with a visitation from the supernatural. Once, many years ago in Florence, I found myself, after dinner with friends, composing in my head a speech in denigration of the prose style of Bernard Levin, at that time Britain's most famous newspaper columnist. I had never met him, but I had seen him on television; and I suppose I might have been a little jealous of the fortune he got paid. The next morning I was crossing the Santa Trinita bridge when I realized that the diminutive figure striding briskly toward me on the same pavement was

Bernard Levin. Such moments, in my experience, can be quite frightening, because they so sharply evoke chance and chaos. Powell's triumph of intuition was to realize, and illustrate, that there are patterns in the chaos; and he thought of all this long before Lorenz and others did the scientific work that established chaos theory. So from that aspect, *A Dance to the Music of Time* is an intellectual feat.

But it's more than that: it's consistently absorbing. Nothing so extended has ever generated such a thirst in the reader for wanting to know what happens next. Will Charles Stringham give way to his alcoholic propensities? Is the beautiful but bitchy Pamela Flitton insane? What will happen to Widmerpool after he marries her? On the level of everyday life among the upper classes the sequence is unbeatable; and always on the understanding that those classes have now been joined by the new people of the literary world and the media in general, so that the old edifice is inevitably crumbling, merely in order that it might become more accommodating.

The great solvent, of course, is World War II, and I now see that nobody ever wrote about it better. Powell spent most of the war as an intelligence officer in London, dealing with representatives of the European countries occupied by the Nazis. He was, therefore, plugged into the future, but he doesn't make a thing of his own role; whereas his friend and rival Evelyn Waugh made much more of his own role than had any relation to fact. Powell was a modest man, although he could be very jealous of his reputation. He would turn on his famous sneer if you raised even the slightest point about a possible fault in any sentence he had ever written. I quickly learned to keep my reservations to myself. Michael Frayn was only one of the fans who thought the last volume of the sequence, *Hearing Secret Harmonies,* was a muffed picture of the so-called Youth Culture, about which Powell knew very little, because he was by then too old to get out amongst it and sample the flavor. But I noticed that Frayn used the soft pedal when he put the opinion in print. The man who wasn't afraid to mock Powell's occasional deficiencies was the late Auberon Waugh, Evelyn Waugh's son: but "Bron" (as everyone called him) overdid it absurdly. He forgot to mention that the whole sequence is an almost unbroken stretch of genius.

New readers should be warned, however, that there is the occasional dull stretch. At the opening of volume 6 (*The Kindly Ones*) there is far too much about servants, ghosts, and the occult. Defending himself against charges that he was too interested in *Burke's Peerage*, Powell once said that he would have been equally interested in a book called *Burke's Workers*. But the truth was that the toffs, or would-be toffs, were what he was best at. And no writer dedicated to showing life as it is should give even fleeting acknowledgment to the occult. The real reason why Scorpio Murtlock, the sinister, hippie-ish cult leader in the last volume, is such an unlikely figure is that Powell gives him a measure of the telepathic power that he claims, whereas in fact the typical counterculture hero was a fake. Evelyn Waugh would not have been fooled for a minute. Nor, probably, would Olivia Manning.

But the really serious fault in Powell's masterpiece is the absence of Americans. In those volumes set in the years between the wars, this absence is already glaring: Mrs. Simpson is allowed to make a fleeting, nameless appearance, but really the rich women of America had for a long time been making inroads into British high society. And in wartime, in Powell's nostalgically remembered London full of foreign uniforms, the absence of American uniforms threatens to turn the whole thing into a fantasy. The shift of power in the direction of the Americans was, after all, a talking point even at the time. Powell's disinclination to even mention it gives the effect of a protective mechanism, a consolation for loss. Powell had a firm understanding of politics: he knew that things would never be the same again. Perhaps he wrote the whole majestic sequence in order to palliate his regret. Like the ruins of an abbey, there is something forlorn about its beauty, an air of desolation that make you glad you have paid the visit, but just as glad not to be staying long. Even its laughter tastes of salt tears.

Though Powell sometimes piled on the subtlety to the point of flirting with the evanescent, he made every other writer purporting to deal with the sweep of British society look crass. This especially applied to C. P. Snow. Snow's novels about the corridors of power (the completed sequence of eleven volumes was called *Strangers and Brothers*) got their grip on the public in the 1950s, a decade before Powell's voice became the established tone in which to talk about the Establishment. (Significantly, the word "Establishment," with its overtones of time-tested authority, came into wide use only as Britain's role as an international administrative system was wound up.) When I was still a student at Sydney University in the late 1950s, to know about Snow's novels was a mark of sophistication. I tried to read them then, and found them so traumatically boring that I can't see myself giving them another try even now. (Part Two: A Decision Is Taken. Chapter One: The Lighting of a Cigarette. It's all like that.) Snow's narrator, Lewis Eliot, talks with the infallibly misplaced emphasis of Powell's Widmerpool. Snow never quite realized that his own pomp and success added up to a comic turn. He was like a walking illustration by Osbert Lancaster, whose name, to me, is still very much alive. All this being said, however, I have noticed that the Penguin volumes of Snow's novels keep cropping up in clusters on Hugh's bookstall. I can just see the moment—though I slightly dread it—when I start assembling a set. But even if they turn out to be more substantial than I once thought, I doubt that those Snow novels that have the academic cloisters for an ambience will be up to the mark later set by David Lodge and Malcolm Bradbury, or even by Tom Sharpe. The academic novel is a genre, and a genre needs to be entertaining. Did Snow ever really entertain anyone? Well, I suppose Sir Walter Scott did, and he wasn't very funny either.

Treasuring Osbert Lancaster

I HAVE ALWAYS thought Osbert Lancaster's little book *Drayneflete Revealed* to be one of the great British comic achievements. Usually, anywhere I lived, I had two copies, one to read and one to give away. Lately I have once again read it through, and marveled as if Lancaster still breathed and had only just now thought of recording Drayneflete's history.

The point of Drayneflete's history is that it isn't up to much. In Roman times it started off as a crossroads of secondary importance and since then, steadily throughout the centuries, one architectural excrescence after another has been added to its agglomeration of mediocrity. These various historical stages and changes of style are recorded in Lancaster's wonderfully conceived illustrations, one of them per chapter, so that each chapter works like a long caption. But the capital joke of the narration is that every step in this long saga of vandalism is presented as if by a spokesman for the current town council, scraping with quiet desperation for any trace of historic interest. The book has the effect of a PR brochure that doesn't know how implausible it is when claiming status and dignity for the kind of progress which is really the gradual destruction of all value. When a hideous new cinema gets built, it is quietly hailed as a brilliant example of the modern style.

What happens to the town happens also to the inhabitants. A few families come down through the centuries. By the twentieth century, the family that forms the center of local society is called de Vere-Tipple. The eldest son, Guillaume de Vere-Tipple, is a poet. In the 1930s, to mark his solidarity with the working class, he calls himself Bill Tipple. He writes a poem about the Spanish Civil War, called "Crack-up in Barcelona." I can confidently recommend it as being a parodic masterpiece in the class of Max Beerbohm. Back in Sydney in the late 1950s, all the would-be writers in my circle were familiar with it, and my late friend Robert Hughes could actually recite the whole thing from memory, without a mistake. I can still see Hughes relishing the last lines about Maxi, the poet's friend, "knocked off the tram by a fascist conductor / who misinterpreted a casual glance."

What Lancaster was saying, when he invented the de Vere-Tipples, was essentially what Thomas Mann was saying when he invented the Buddenbrooks: a grand family forfeits its power when its younger generation gets more interested in the arts than in business. But Lancaster treated the theme in a small space, glancingly. In his prose as in his graphics, compression and suggestion were his best tricks. (He did stage sets that could suggest whole eras, and they were all done as simple painted flats, with no machinery: a triumph of stylistic accuracy.) In command of encyclopedic knowledge of the history of the arts and the applied arts, he could weave a texture out of nothing but allusions to what he knew. In that way his writings remind you of Patrick Leigh Fermor, whose key book *A Time of Gifts* I have just bought off the stall for my elder daughter. I might borrow it from her when she has finished it and read it yet again: the paragraphs evoking his first walk in the Wachau valley of the Danube are like poems. But although I possess all of Lancaster's books, including two copies of the marvelous *Home Sweet Homes*, I had for some reason never read his slim volume of reminiscence about the years between the wars, *With an Eye to the Future*. Now that I am at last reading it, I don't want it to end. Here are all the originals for the people in Betjeman, Evelyn Waugh, Nancy Mitford, and Anthony Powell. Here are the stately homes, the London flats, the evening clothes, the cars, the drinks. In the wonderful illustrations, sometimes bled out to a full page, you can see the teeming population of marginal cultural figures mentioned in the text: that fat-faced gourmand must be Cyril Connolly, and that exquisite young man with the snooty profile must be Brian Howard, the almost entirely poisonous aesthete who later went on to write one of my favorite poems, "Gone to Report."

As I read, I can feel it all slipping away into time as I am myself. Probably all this stuff—this last stretch of a privileged social history—will never again come back into favor. Perhaps we loved reading about it out there in the colonies only because we, the colonized, were even more reluctant than the imperialists to let go of a dying empire. John Carey, the cleverest of all critics in a generation of clever critics, has always hated that whole self-consciously arty era, to the point of arguing that it wasn't artistic at all. He thought that all good things were in the grip of a

lucky elite, and needed to be prized loose. He was probably right. Certainly the whole cozy shebang is hard to explain to Americans, who live in a proclaimed democracy,
and not in a stratified society whose top layer gives up its
advantages as slowly as it can. But even Carey was obliged,
when picking out his fifty most enjoyable books of the
twentieth century, to admit that Waugh's *Decline and Fall*
was one of them. It's one of the good things about the
study of literature: taste trumps prejudice. I feel the same
way about Osbert Lancaster's lineup of slim volumes: I
ought to disapprove, but I can't leave them alone.

American Power

I FIRST BOUGHT and read David Halberstam's *The Powers That Be* in Washington, in 1980. On assignment from the *Observer*, and faced with such daunting tasks as interviewing Zbigniew Brzezinski, I needed books that would explain the American political system to me as concisely as possible. In his knowledgeable analysis of how the power structure of the media related to the power structure of the nation—the newspapers were still instrumental in those days, but television was already becoming a preponderant element—Halberstam helped to form my taste for reading about American politics. Reading the book again now, I am usefully reminded that the sainthood of William Paley was questionable. Contrary to legend, it wasn't the CBS news programmes, with Ed Murrow to the fore, that undid McCarthy; and Paley not only ensured that Murrow was kept on a taut leash, he eventually got rid of him altogether. Paley's supposedly ethical empire turned stupid in order to expand: an edemic declension that he encouraged, having deduced, correctly, that in America his prestige would be enhanced the more power he took. All this was laid out well by Halberstam, and it still reads like essential news. Unfortunately, one is also once again reminded that Halberstam, so diligent in his research, was hopelessly careless at the level of constructing a sentence. It wasn't as if he couldn't write at all: he could, but only a breath at a time. Clauses were botched together with no thought for grammatical continuity. Today, his scrappy paragraphs look so clumsy that I wonder why, at the time, I wasn't put off American political writing altogether.

But others wrote better, and anyway the subject was too rich to leave alone. About power in the media, Ken Auletta has written a whole string of thrilling books about which conglomerate merged with which, and dozens of books such as Timothy Crouse's *The Boys on the Bus* bring you the very smell of the political reporters crammed onto the zoo plane and behaving more and more badly as they slog away at translating press handouts into printable copy. As for power in Washington, by now there are enough essential books to keep you going forever, or anyway to make you redefine the word "essential." I went on to read all the many books about Washington by Elizabeth Drew, and at least one book—*The Wise Men,* by Walter Isaacson and Evan Thomas—opened up for me the huge subject of how American politics affected the whole world, and vice versa. Essentially such books were journalism, but they were also proof that journalism is the first draft of formal history. And sometimes, of course, it was the journalists, not the professors, who wrote the formal history that counted: William Shirer's *The Rise and Fall of the Third Reich* might have begun as a report by a journalist on the spot, but as a history of its subject it was never been equaled, nor is it likely to be.

Reading about American politics was as thrilling, and almost as much fun, as reading about Hollywood. Even today I usually read the latest book by Bob Woodward as soon as it comes out, even though I find him a pedestrian writer, and his book about John Belushi, *Wired,* was so misleading—he treated the crack-up of a comedian as if it were the fall of a president—that it made me suspect the emotional veracity (not the veracity: he checks his facts until they weep with boredom) of everything Woodward has written since. Nor is Woodward fully at home when writing about the American Establishment, even though he has long been a co-opted member of it. British students of American political writing would prefer to believe that in America there is much less emphasis on social background. In fact there is at least as much. It not only helps us if we know exactly what the words mean when we are told that the young George W. Bush was tapped for Skull and Bones; it also helps us if we know that part of Nixon's paranoia about the Kennedy family had an understandable basis in social resentment. He thought that JFK had been born to the purple, and that the patriarch of the family, old Joe Kennedy, was the kind of man against whom it was wise to get your retaliation in first. He was quite right about that.

Sally Bedell Smith's *Grace and Power,* a chronicle of the JFK White House, is an example of the Higher Gossip: always a suspect genre, because we tend to enjoy it too much. I bought the book new, from Heffer's in Trinity Street: an act of extravagance justifiable because I thought it would make a good birthday present for my younger daughter, who has an uncanny ability to race through a factual book and retain every fact in it, thereby steadily replenishing herself in the role of a walking encyclopedia available for consultation to the entire family. The book, she reported, was an ace effort. I borrowed it back from her and soon found that she was right. Sally Bedell Smith has Kitty Kelley's gift for getting at the real story behind the glamour, but she does a better job of bringing everything to the level of historic significance, instead of lowering it to the level of triviality. JFK's compulsive womanizing is not scamped: indeed it is the central subject. (In a real book about his presidency, the central subject would be his politics, but this is a book about the man himself, whom Bedell Smith insists, correctly in my opinion, on locating within the pattern of his private behavior.) But if JFK emerges as a satyr, his wife Jackie does not emerge as a patsy. This is one of the best accounts I have read of her formidable stature. Usually any written portrait of her, especially if the work of a woman, makes her out as a fashion plate, even when the high levels of her taste and knowledge are conceded. Bedell makes the taste and knowledge the center of her story. She was the perfect consort for JFK in his imperial role. He knew it, but he betrayed her anyway. It wasn't just that he couldn't help it; he didn't want to help it, even for a moment.

The press knew but said nothing, just as they had

known about FDR's paralysis but never mentioned it. In later times—which can be said to have started the moment after JFK was shot—his behavior would have got him either fired, or, more probably, never elected. Bill Clinton got into a Watergate-sized scandal over an adulterous episode that ranked nowhere beside JFK's least frolic. But JFK didn't just have the advantage of living in an era when the administration was still able to control the twenty-four-hour news cycle: most of his women were of a classy background and thus not susceptible to being hired by the press to spill the beans. That being said, however, there was nothing upmarket about Judith Campbell, the mistress he shared with the mobster Sam Giancana. Not much further in the future, such an alliance would have dished him.

The story is intoxicating but raises the question of whether we ought to be intoxicated. Perhaps not, but abstention would not be easy. Gossip of such quality (at these altitudes, as the Spanish say) feels like the food of life, as if hors d'oeuvres could be the whole meal. And if the caviar and the blinis are good enough, why eat anything else? Well, knowing how many new young women the glowing American prince could get through in a week won't tell you how he got Khrushchev to take the missiles out of Cuba. There is a bigger picture. But to do her credit, our author knows about that too, and is able to set JFK's priapic energies within a truly historical context. So finally this is an essential book about American politics. The story about François Hollande's entanglement with the enchantress Julie Gayet—it was still going on while I was reading about JFK's heroic efforts to marshal the supply of secretaries who joined him in the White House swimming pool—would be an essential book about French politics, but less sensational in its effect, because in France these things are well understood. In America, what is well understood is that they are not allowed. Among his many deleterious medical conditions, JFK had at least one that threatened his life, but nobody in the Kennedy family, and not one staff member, ever told the press. In *The West Wing*, President Bartlet has a similarly serious chronic ailment, and the whole plot of almost the entire multiseason serial turns on the fact that the ailment has been concealed. But what Bartlet was not allowed to have, even in supposedly more enlightened times, was a secret habit involving women. Nobody would have watched. In that respect, the American TV culture, impressive though it has become, is still outstripped by books.

Gripped by a specific hunger for huge American books that deal with the new imperialism—which is a cultural imperialism, beyond the power of armies—I moved directly to *Personal History*, the autobiography of Katharine Graham, which I should have read in 1997, when it first came out. At the time, Kay Graham was still well in charge of the whole *Washington Post* conglomerate, including *Newsweek* and the TV stations: the proprietress had become the hands-on administrator, and therefore one of the most powerful women in America. She wrote the book in the full confidence conferred by her position. But what makes the book so good is that she remembers a time when she was not confident at all. It lasted for all of her childhood and much of her adulthood. She had an overwhelming mother, and later she was plunged into an overwhelming world.

Briefly, it can be said that she was born and raised in a context where women were supposed to be dainty and attractive, and she always felt like a lump. Even her mother, who did all kinds of extracurricular things including translating Thomas Mann, was basically a glamour puss: i.e., not a lump. That Kay Graham–née–Meyer's lack of routine glamour worked her way in the end is easy to say now. Had she been the standard-issue high-society debutante, she might have gone on to consume her mature years as a wife, mother, and hostess of many accomplishments. She might have had the life that seemed set down for Jacqueline Lee Bouvier before she, too, went looking for a real personality of her own, instead of just a standard screenplay. But Kay Meyer, as inside the system of rich connections as a woman could be, felt like an outsider. She was a wallflower, and her nervousness made her ill. In the book she is disturbingly frank about how unsettling it felt. Another strength of her account is that she is fully aware that her anguish of uncertainty is bound to seem like self-indulgence in a context where so many American women were too poor to choose their lives. Such a realization added embarrassment to uncertainty. She wasn't Cinderella: she belonged at the ball. That was just the trouble. She belonged; but she was not, by her own estimation, qualified. She could feel the eyes of a whole social stratum on her, finding her inadequate.

The book is the long and sometimes sad story of how she attained a sense of qualification. It was a social milieu in which men ruled. It was taken for granted that her brilliant husband, Phil Graham, would run things, although he did not own them. As well as running the Empire, Phil was the one who had the entrée into the Kennedy administration's Camelot on the Potomac. Kay was just the wife. To do her credit, she was not content with this; and to do some of the men credit, they were in her corner. Ben Bradlee, as editor of the *Washington Post*, behaved especially well. With Bradlee's help she gradually asserted herself until, after Phil's suicide, she was ready to adopt the burden of command. I wonder why the book is not more often cited by feminists: perhaps too many of them are too far on the left, and don't believe that a poor little rich girl can have real problems. In chapter 21, she gives an especially touching account of how women of her class were pressured to belittle themselves in order to fit into a man's world. She fought back well, and eventually she was ready to resist even the tawdry might of the Nixon administration, which pulled every conceivable dirty trick in order to persuade her to call off the *Post*'s investigations of the Watergate caper. Woodward and Bernstein could not have done without the support of Bradlee, but Bradlee could not have done without the support of Kay Graham. The Nixon people—with the aid of the Justice Department, which was in their pocket—were ready to burn down the whole of the *Washington Post* empire. The constitution would not have been enough to stop them. It took the guts of the proprietress. In her brainy integrity, the great lady reminds you of Eleanor Roosevelt, who was no glamour girl either, but was still the center of attention. Kay Graham and Adlai Stevenson used to see a lot of each other. Their conversation must have been fascinating. Unfortunately, there are no tape recordings of it. We only have tapes of Nixon.

Kipling and the Widow-maker

BACK IN 2010, during my first year of illness, I added to my woes by stupidly contriving to remain immobile in my cabin throughout an Atlantic crossing to New York, instead of walking around the deck a few times each day as I should have done. It rained all the way, but that was no excuse, because on a ship as big as the *Queen Mary 2* you can do a satisfactory deck walk just by using the internal corridors. Instead, I did a long lie-down, and paid the penalty by finding out, when I arrived in New York, that I had contracted a thrombosis. After ten days in Mount Sinai hospital there was the long trip back to England, and even then I was not free of the effects. The price of safety from a further occurrence, I was told, lay in Ambulation. The doctors managed to pronounce the word with a capital "A," and I still do so myself. Every day I Ambulate for at least half an hour, to make sure that my legs get some work to do. In the summer months the walk to town and back counts as Ambulation. I Ambulate to the bookshops, load up with a few books, and Ambulate back again. But in cold or wet weather, Ambulation must be done inside the house. It felt like a perfect waste of time until I hit upon the device of reading while I Ambulated. All I needed was a fair mental map of where the furniture was and I could Ambulate while reading Kipling's poetry. It seemed a fitting activity because so many of his poems are written in a kind of march rhythm. They are soldierly stuff.

And yet, how brilliant. Technically, he could do anything. Here is the whole of his little four-line epic "The Sleepy Sentinel."

> Faithless the watch I kept: now I have none to keep.
> I was slain because I slept; now I am slain I sleep.
> Let no man reproach me again, whatever watch is
>   unkept—
> I sleep because I am slain. They slew me because I
>   slept.

The trouble with the owner of the technique that can do anything is that he is continually tempted to do everything at once. Left to their own impulses, his poems make so much noise that they seldom settle into the condition of a statement: they are always giving you a whole symphony. Yet one must confess to a certain relief that so many of Kipling's poems rule themselves out: whether because they are burdened by too much dialect, or too much flashy wordplay, they usefully tell us that we need not go back to them. If he had reined himself in, he would have been a poet the way he was a writer of short stories: one of the supreme exponents in the language. Even as things are, with your capacity for attention automatically whittling down the number of his poems that you would wish to revisit— and perhaps your capacity for attention is declining any- way—there is more than enough of him to keep you mur- muring with admiration. He has the knack, peculiar to the poetic genius, of speaking in your own throat. It would be the wish of any poet to attain the phonetic force of the first stanza of "Harp Song of the Dane Women."

> What is a woman that you forsake her,
> And the hearth fire and the home-acre,
> To go with the old grey Widow-maker?

Unforgettable for the power of its movement, the whole poem is like that. If that one poem had ten companions, he would have changed the history of English poetry. But of course it has, scattered about in his works; and he almost did. It's just that his influence proved impossible to absorb. Kipling deserves all the praise he gets from Craig Raine's introductory essay to *Rudyard Kipling: Selected Poems*, a Penguin of the perfect weight and dimensions for the Ambulatory student. T. S. Eliot once did a good selection too, with an essay presaging Raine's in its analytical approval. Both Eliot and Raine, inventors of their own manner, can be seen struggling, however elegantly, with the self-imposed task of coaxing a raging bull into the back of a small truck. The urge, for any poet who reads Kipling, is to get his energy under control before it infects everybody with the ruinous urge to emulate him.

Speer in Spandau

WHEN HE WAS IN Spandau prison, Albert Speer walked long distances to stay in shape. He calculated the number of paces to Istanbul, checked off the number of paces he walked each day in the prison yard, and eventually, without having left Berlin, he reached his destination. Later on he got as far as Beijing. It's one of the more believable stories in his book *Spandau: The Secret Diaries,* which I have just read again. This time I read it in English, although there was a day when I could read it fairly easily in German. All his books are good for your German, but I am not at all sure they are good for your soul. As a writer, he never let up on his act as the civilized man, the true artist, who got caught up in the dream world of the fake artist Hitler because it offered such irresistible aesthetic opportunities.

The message being, you might have been him. To deny this, you have to be unembarrassed about speaking with a confidence that feels like bluster. But surely he was pulling a fast one, which he made all the more persuasive by pulling it slowly. Over the years, after the war, both in prison and out, he told the world that he should have known what the Nazis were up to, and could not forgive himself for his ignorance. But he did know, and he was never ignorant. He was especially vulnerable on that last point because he liked to be seen as the man who knew everything. He resolved the paradox by a quietly histrionic trick of looking puzzled at all times, as if those big questions were too much even for a man with such a fine taste in tailoring. In the movie *Downfall* he is chiefly present as a model for black leather overcoats, but we are asked yet again to believe that when Hitler ordered him to destroy the remains of Germany's infrastructure, Speer disobeyed the order, in the interest of future generations. His account of how he defied Hitler's order was probably at least partly true, but confidence is not increased by the fact that his account of how little he knew about the Final Solution was at least partly a lie. Still, his guilt remains a personal question for all of us who were alive in those years, even if we were not born until near the very end of them. What would we have done? Something to ponder while we, too, go walking to Beijing.

Shakespeare and Johnson

WHEN I STILL DID a lot of traveling to make TV shows or appear on stage, I always took my complete Shakespeare with me on a long flight. It was the old Selfridge's one-volume edition, with no notes but with an excellent introduction by Sir Henry Irving himself. Thus, because I was always traveling, I was always reading Shakespeare, even when the book fell to pieces so seriously that it had to be held together with a rubber band. In particular I read the history plays and the tragedies. The comedies I have always been able to read less often, although *A Midsummer Night's Dream* is a special case. I like to read it every couple of years. Recently, on a midsummer night, I went with the family to see an open-air production in King's College gardens. For my granddaughter, aged eight, it was the second time she had seen the play, and during the interval she politely made it clear that she had seen it done better: a knowledgeable theatergoer. She was right, alas. The production was uninspired. Though they were hired-in professionals and not the usual bunch of mistakenly confident undergraduates, only a few of the actors knew how to speak. But the lines survived the beating they took. The text is a crowd pleaser, however transmitted. Hence the obvious answer to Johnson's momentary puzzlement in his note on the play, when he quotes the bit about "the fiery glow-worm's eyes" and says "I know not how Shakespeare, who commonly derived his knowledge of nature from his own observation, happened to place the glow-worm's light in his eyes, which is only in his tail." But Shakespeare wasn't just interested in what he himself knew to be true: he was interested in what the audience thought to be true, as they sat there and watched. As always, however, I would rather have been reading than watching.

Time having gone by since I fell ill, I have become reconciled to never traveling very far again, so I need a new routine for reading Shakespeare. I have taken to keeping a single volume of the Arden Shakespeare on my writing desk in the kitchen. At the moment it is *Antony and Cleopatra*. The Roman plays are my favorite Shakespeare anyway, and *Antony and Cleopatra* is my second-favorite among those—after *Julius Caesar*—so this is a high-ranking event. I have just finished going through the volume line by line and footnote by footnote, with increasing admiration for M. R. Ridley, who brought R. H. Case's 1906 edition up to date with modern scholarship: modern for 1954. I spent decades getting familiar with Shakespeare without resorting to footnotes, but it was a doomed forgoing. Eventually you must look at the footnotes or you won't know where you are. It remains true, however, that the best moments hit you without benefit of clergy. In *Antony and Cleopatra*, T. S. Eliot thought that the line most worth talking about comes from Charmian when she dies: "Ah, soldier!" I have always thought that Eliot was right, and now I still do. Charmian has so little to say at the crucial moment, and the soldier, of course, has even less. But it is the way the words are placed. The handmaiden's transition into death was almost nothing, a pinprick: and yet for her it was a revelation. How great the great poet was, to know that.

Shakespeare brings me to Johnson's notes on Shakespeare, which form a neat and abundant little book, *Johnson on Shakespeare*, edited for Oxford University Press by Walter Raleigh in 1908; but you need a volume containing the revisions made in 1925. Only a couple of hundred pages long but with something memorable said in every paragraph, almost in every sentence, it makes an ideal book for holding in front of your nose while you pace up and down the kitchen. Johnson is so good when he comments on poetry that anybody who comments on his comments usually has little to add. His gift for pertinence needs to be remembered when the reader picks up either of the two small Oxford volumes of his *Lives of the Poets* and is dismayed to find that so many of the names in the list of contents are unrecognizable. Johnson had good things to say about Milton and Dryden, but he also had good things to say about Smith.

Yes, there was a poet called Smith, and the details of his life were almost as little known then as they are now. But Smith had a certain renown for his poetic abilities, and Johnson did not disagree. Johnson said that Smith had all the talents, but achieved nothing with them. That observation reminds me of some of my fellow writers, when I was young, who were so gifted that they practically had to fight to achieve obscurity. Late in my life I still find it remarkable that they attained their aim. Johnson's specific criticism, full of detail about technical points, abounds with general topics that lead you into questions about the creative life. Nor was "Dictionary Johnson" ever quite the strict academician that you might have expected from his reputation for whipping the ignorant. He was just as much descriptive as he was prescriptive. He observed the growth and change of language for what it was: a living thing. "That our language is in perpetual danger of corruption," he wrote in his Life of Roscommon, "cannot be denied; but what prevention can be found? The present manners of the nation would deride authority, and therefore nothing is left but that every writer should criticise himself." All he needed to add was that unless you can criticize yourself, you are not a writer.

Naipaul's Nastiness

A MODERNIZING force embattled against his own background, V. S. Naipaul is the Kemal Ataturk of the Indian subcontinent. He has always wanted the Indian culture that he came from—by way of Trinidad—to be modernized, if necessary out of existence. Or so, for most of his life, he seemed to say. He rousingly, and wittily, declared himself against the caste system, but in his later days he often proved that he was still an unreconstructed Brahmin: once, at his home in London, a workman wanted his help in opening a window, and Naipaul telephoned his wife at her place of work to tell her that he was being disturbed, and could she come home immediately because there was manual labor to be done. Or so the legend goes: with him there are always legends, increasingly boosted, in the autumn of patriarchy, by his own testimony. He behaved like an autocrat to his women, and in 2008 he cooperated with

a biography saying that he did. Throughout his writing
career, some of his most entertaining stuff has been written in contempt of the backwardness of the culture from
which his family fought to emerge. He can be hilarious
about just how little cleaning an Indian cleaner gets done
when cleaning the steps of a government building, but
perhaps the hilarity would be less hilarious if you were an
Indian. Nevertheless, we read Naipaul for his fastidious
scorn, not for his large heart. Like the comparably great
Nirad Chaudhuri, he is supreme for his style as a writer
in English, not for his profundity as an Indian thinker.
His self-taught father—a minor local journalist in many
ways even more admirable than his relatively privileged
son—had shared the same priorities, if not the same talent. In a handsome Vintage paperback which I collared
from Hugh's bookstall, *Between Father and Son* collects
the correspondence between the two men during the years
when young Vidia was in Oxford, a scholarship boy like
any other, except that he was an Indian. His father, his
mother, and all his close relatives expected regular letters
from him. This demand he did his best to supply, without
even hinting that he had essays to write for his tutors and it
would be a blessing if he could relax in his spare hours. But

the real measure of his stifling family context was given by what happened when a letter to him from an English girlfriend mistakenly got sent to Trinidad. It was immediately opened. The whole family read it and made comments. He was unable adequately to express his dismay. Later on he would get better at expressing it, but that was how his invigorating apostasy began: in the very aspects of close family life that seem to us so enviable, but which would have suffocated us had they been our own fate.

With these beginnings of his glittering career in mind, I have taken down from my shelves a copy of his *Literary Occasions* that I bought in New York in 2004, in the days when I could scarcely visit the Strand bookshop without spending a thousand dollars. (By the time the parcels of books reached London I had forgotten what was in them, so the whole deal worked out like Christmas squared.)

One of the occasions is a wonderful essay about Conrad, called "Conrad's Darkness and Mine."

Naipaul talks about Conrad's analysis of the colonial experience. In doing so, Naipaul talks about his own colonial experience. And in reading Naipaul on that subject, I am faced with *my* colonial experience, and brought to realize how complex it has all been, this birth, growth, and breaking up of an empire. And most of it happened so abruptly. After a few hundred years' practice in subjugating Ireland, the British subjugated most of the world in the blinking of an eye. Now there is nothing left except a language, a golden coach, and a few pipers marching and countermarching in the courtyard of Edinburgh castle. Eventually we might even have to say goodbye to Scotland, and there will be nothing of the old imperial world left except ten square yards of sand in Belize. Naipaul at his best, as a writer of factual narrative, gives you the sense that the language itself is the imperial inheritance that matters. Whether I shall read *A House for Mr Biswas* again remains to be seen. More than fifty years ago it filled me with admiration, but reminded me too much of the house where I was born.

Movie Books

ONCE AGAIN I HAVE read, right through the length of its hefty bulk, *My Indecision Is Final,* by Jake Eberts and Terry Ilott. The story of one of Britain's several doomed attempts to have its own Hollywood-style film industry, it really should be a bit of a downer. Goldcrest, the British company in question, had one of the biggest hit movies ever, *Gandhi:* but it still went broke. Eberts was the executive in charge and really the whole thing was his fault, so why take him as an expert? Why am I always reading his book? Not just because it is one of the best books about the movies, but because it is one of the best books about show business in general. Many of us who have lived and flourished in show business are reluctant to admit that we have no talent for it. What we are good at is the arts: the strategic commercial sense that makes the arts possible is quite beyond us. *My Indecision Is Final* does a wonderful job of analyzing how the movies need an industrial effort and that if you can't do the industry bit you shouldn't start. I suppose if Eberts had been really good at industry, he would never have had a catastrophe to report and the book would not have been written. But he was good enough at it to be able to lay out the relevant factors in a thrilling linkage of cause and effect.

Goldcrest made some good movies. *The Mission* is still worth a look, even if only because Robert De Niro is such a walking definition of screen stardom that he merely has to flex his jaw in a determined manner, while Jeremy Irons has to act his head off. Nor did *The Mission* lose money at the same rate as *The Emerald Forest,* although both movies taken together added up to yet another lesson (long ago learned by Hollywood) that you should never go filming in the jungle unless you can build the jungle in a studio. And then there was *Gandhi,* the dream product that won Oscars and made zillions: money and prestige, Goldcrest had them both.

But in the film business, prestige never earns enough on its own. The overheads will eat you up unless you can maintain a flow of ordinary product. In Britain the home market simply isn't big enough to sustain a steady effort for anything more ambitious than the brain-dead *Carry On* series, so all you can have is the occasional outburst of talented people managing to convince the banks that this time things will be different. Sometimes they are; Ealing Studios, for example, was the creation of a man of genius, Sir Michael Balcon; but just for that reason, it lasted no longer than he did. Avowedly aspiring to be something more solidly based than a one-man show, Goldcrest was awash with talent but it couldn't do anything normal, and all too soon the dream died. One is faced with the sad possibility that the main reason why the book is so enjoyable is schadenfreude. It can be fun to watch such clever people run their heads into a wall.

The same might apply to *Final Cut*, Steven Bach's book about the pretentious fiasco that was *Heaven's Gate*, Michael Cimino's fanatically authentic, and therefore hideously expensive, re-creation of a Wild West range war that never happened in the first place. On behalf of United Artists, Steven Bach was the executive in charge: a suit with a proven brain. So really, in writing his account of how it all went wrong, he was in the same position as Jake Eberts at Goldcrest. The book is a piercing character study of Michael Cimino, from which the reader is forced to conclude that Cimino never had a character at all. He was a chameleon with delusions of grandeur. He lied like Hemingway—he invented a role for himself in the Green Berets in the same way that Hemingway invented a role for himself in the Arditi—and operated on the principle that if you disagreed with him about anything you must have been working with the enemy. But some of his delusions were convincing: hence the perfection of the trap into which Bach and the other UA executives so worthily walked, convinced that Cimino was a great film artist. To do them, and him, credit, he had already provided the world with what looked like proof that this might be true. His movie *The Deer Hunter* was such a huge hit, both critical and commercial, that he was hailed as an avatar.

Prestige and money: that dangerous double score. The paradox underlying the whole mad project of *Heaven's Gate* was that the studio got into it because the executives believed in art. If Cimino had not been carrying his wealth of laurels as an artist, and promising to add to them, his big idea for the range war epic would never have got off the ground—or, at least, never gone on location. But off he and his vast crew went to Montana, where they had already set fire to a hill of money before a single camera turned. A large piece of Montana Cimino bought for himself, on the studio's tab. Long ago, Erich von Stroheim taught Hollywood how hard it is to stop a runaway production. United Artists might also have drawn on the example of the Anglo-French Concorde supersonic airliner project, which was unstoppable for the same reason: when you have spent so much, it becomes impossible to write it off. But Bach's rueful narrative is a demonstration of how it is possible to understand every stage of a disaster and still be forced to go along with it to the end.

It ended in bad reviews and an empty box office. I still remember seeing it, and feeling my life growing shorter in a way that I don't feel even now, when it is. After the smoke cleared, United Artists was in ruins and Michael Cimino changed gender. Steven Bach went on to write this marvelous book. His book about Leni Riefenstahl is also very good, although I won't be reading it again: her movies were monstrous, but so was she, so there was no discrepancy between aim and result, and hence no lesson. *Heaven's Gate* was all lessons; and today, in its afterlife, it exists on no other level. The strangest and most long-lasting of the lessons, however, was that some of the critics managed to convince themselves that a shapeless movie—and not just shapeless in its general outline, but shapeless from scene to scene—was some kind of masterpiece. There have been several attempts to resuscitate the reputation that it justly never earned. One concludes that in the field of movie criticism there is a sucker born every minute. Were he still alive, Steven Bach would have the grace to say that the same applies to movie executives. Since his book came out in 1985 I have taken pleasure in recommending it to anyone who shows signs of being interested in the popular arts, or, indeed, in any kind of arts at all.

Women in Hollywood

ONE OF THE encouraging developments in Hollywood in recent times has been the rise to influence of women behind the camera. Hollywood will always be a sinkhole of cupidity, but there are some respects in which justice pays, and women were unlikely to be held back forever in a context where talent can be translated into cash. (A big difference, there, between Los Angeles and Saudi Arabia.) In *Hello, He Lied* the producer Lynda Obst gives us a lesson in what intelligence and sensitivity can do when combined with the near-military practical sense needed to organize a movie. This is the second time I have read her book and I enjoyed it even more than the first time, perhaps because by now the trend she helped to inaugurate looks like part of the atmosphere, instead of just another rebellion that might wither and die. (The career of Ida Lupino used to be cited as a trend, until it was sadly realized that the trend consisted of one person.) Especially in the television branch of the filming world, women's names are now everywhere among the leading credits; and in the film branch, even though it is still a jungle, not everyone behind a powerful desk is a male gorilla; some of them are female gorillas, and much more fastidious in their habits. Obst is very good on the subject of the diligence required to take meetings and phone calls all day long. *Sleepless in Seattle* is one of her projects: the movie stays good, but one of the reasons is that she was good at phone calls.

Similarly, in the film world a meeting is a civilized battle, but there is no point to being civilized if you can't fight in the first place. To that extent, she is not ladylike; but only if you think that ladies should sit still to be overruled. The only element missing from her gift for the useful rule of thumb ("Never go to a meeting without a strategy") is that she is not especially funny. Lighthearted, yes: but not hilarious. Julia Phillips, who pioneered the format of the female executive *vade mecum* with her brilliantly entertaining *You'll Never Eat Lunch in This Town Again,* was hilarious. Reading it again, I find that her book still is, though more than ever it generates too great a sense of waste. The producer of *Taxi Driver, The Sting,* and *Close Encounters* could have done even more: run studios, run for president. But the cocaine got her. Sometimes I think I might have been a Puritan all along. I drank too much, smoked cigarettes and cigars like an idiot, and at one period I was the kind of pothead who looked like a small cloud being propelled by a pair of legs. But even in my present condition I still tend to draw myself up to my full height and denounce all users of hard drugs. They are such an unequivocal attack on the brain. Julia Phillips was brilliant and funny and could write a book. She was Nora Ephron and Elaine May rolled into one. How dared she throw all that on the fire? In her book she talks quite a lot about her sad proclivities, but the more she confesses, the less confidence the reader has in her when she touches on other topics. Would you buy a movie about aliens from somebody whose idea of solving her personal problems is to cram Peru up her nose?

Despite the ruinous consequence of Julia Phillips's coke habit, women have gone on to something like equality in Hollywood, and sometimes, intermittently, to something like dominance. In 2008 a remake of George Cukor's 1939 movie *The Women* appeared, based, like its predecessor, on the stage play by Clare Boothe Luce. Diane English, who wrote, produced, and directed the remake, spent fifteen years of her life setting it up. The movie not only is the brainchild of a woman, it stars nothing but women, and even the extras are all women. Unfortunately, the result is utterly unwatchable. Feminism is an ideology, and like any other ideology it can easily transmute a necessary perception into an indulgent madness. The studio heads sat on the movie, on the sensible principle that nobody except an idiot would want to see it, but finally their nerve cracked and they released it. What was wrong with the idea? A world without men doesn't look like the world, however desirable the notion might sometimes seem. For once, the studio bigwigs should have stuck to their conservative instincts.

Still, Hollywood tales of fallibility add up to a field of interest that can never lose its charm. I reread a few pages of David McClintick's *Indecent Exposure*, which recounts how the film executive David Begelman embezzled ten thousand dollars belonging to the actor Cliff Robertson; and I soon found myself rereading it all. Begelman didn't need to embezzle money: he earned millions. He embezzled because one of his many talents was a talent for the shortcut, and he thought that if Cliff Robertson's bank account was open for pilfering, then it ought to be pilfered:

it was practically a duty, an act of morality. Robertson was a wealthy man beyond his high fees for stardom, but he also had the strange characteristic of honesty. The collision of Robertson's strange characteristic with Begelman's strange characteristic made for a story begging to be told, and McClintick tells it well, with the proviso that he is the kind of writer who can't tell "flaunt" from "flout" and who must therefore feign the literacy that he would like to embody.

But a few solecisms don't much hurt the story, which is essentially an illustration of how, in Hollywood, a mighty figure need not fall, even when he is caught with his hand in the bag. Begelman was forgiven by the industry, whose illuminati thought that he must have been sick, or else he would have embezzled serious money instead of just a lousy few thousand dollars. If anyone emerged from the affair with his reputation damaged, it was Cliff Robertson, for making such a fuss.

Essentially all the stories of Hollywood fallibility are the one story, differing only in who tells it best. The interesting news is not so much that weak men, when given power, are still weak, but that whole empires of production have been built up which incorporate human corruptibil-

ity, allow for it, and even thrive on it. Books which analyze
the durability of the Hollywood imperial systems are thus
almost as interesting as books which analyze its frailty. Really the studios have never been frail at all: it might seem
that a great brand name can be brought low by a single
bad choice—Fox almost ruined by *Cleopatra*, UA totally
ruined by *Heaven's Gate*—but in fact the structures under-
went decades of early testing and usually could be shaken
only when it made business sense to merge or be absorbed.

Hollywood is a scale model of corporate America.
Soon I will once again read *The Genius of the System*, by
Thomas Schatz. I can tell I will, because I never really stop
reading it. Exhaustively researched in the studio archives,
the book shows how the survival of any filmmaking enterprise depended on Poverty Row: there had to be ordinary
product to make the money, so that the occasional extraordinary product could aim at prestige, and thus act as a
loss leader even when it failed. It was all worked out before sound was invented. And although many of the men
who built the system loved the movies, they could just as
well have been selling gloves. Most of them were Jews, as
Neal Gabler describes in *An Empire of Their Own*. Good
at finance, they used their expertise to move into a business

territory that didn't yet exist. It was a collective act of imagination, which would attain such an all-pervasive reality that we can't now imagine our lives without it. My own business has always been with serious books, yet I have spent a large proportion of my life—years, when you add it up—watching movies and their television derivatives, and a lot of the books I have read have been about those movies. Some of them felt like a waste of time, but usually I felt as if I was learning something, unless the book was devoted to the kind of film theory that briefly surfaced in the 1960s and struck anyone intelligent as simply begging to be ignored. (The word "semiotics" was always a tip-off: head for the hills!) When I classify film books now, as time gets tighter, I ask myself whether the book is likely to contain anything I don't know already. I have just read Tom Shone's lavishly illustrated monograph on *Scorsese*. Shone writes well, but I would probably not have read his book if I hadn't been asked to review it; whereas his wide-ranging treatise *Blockbuster* is a book I would like to read again. Books that give you the cultural scope of Hollywood are valuable right up the point when it is some sub–Frankfurt School pundit writing them, and even then, Otto Friedrich's *City of Nets*, written from a lofty

European viewpoint, is full of crunchy moments. (It was Friedrich who revealed to me that in California during the Nathanael West period there was a cult fad billing itself as Brain Breathing: The Secret of the Aztecs.) The glossy book in a large format, on the other hand, is rarely worth the effort of lifting it. David Thomson's *Moments That Made the Movies* ranks nowhere beside his often-revised *Biographical Dictionary of Film*, which is even more batso but at least gives you a shower of judgments you can argue with. On that level, film books are a way of quarrelling while alone. They are popcorn reading for people who are glad not to have to share their popcorn. I exempt from this stricture any collection of pieces by a proper film critic such as David Denby or (the incomparable, in my view) Anthony Lane, but I wonder whether the collection of critical journalism, as a form, might not die with the print media. If so, it could live again on the web. As a print journalist who still remembers the sweet smell of hot metal, I would like to think that my principal means of expression will not survive my passing, but the truth is that nothing stops the kids. On my own website I have provided a gateway (in the Web section) to a blog called *Self-Styled Siren*. Sane in judgment and global in scope, the Siren, whose real name is Farran Nehme, seems to have seen every movie in the world. Even more annoyingly, she writes like an ace. You can cruise her site for a long time before remembering that time is not infinite, even though the love of art might seem to make it so.

Extra Shelves

WHEN IS AN EXTRA bookshelf not really an extra book-shelf? When you don't have to build it. In my house I am under steady pressure from my most frequent visitors—wife, two daughters—not to turn it into a book warehouse like every other dwelling I have ever been in. Some of my critics are shameless in this regard. In my wife's ex-tended kitchen there are piles of books which have been there for years. Her magnificent scholarly library extends in an orderly manner through several rooms, but some-how it reaches the kitchen as Antarctic ice reaches the sea. Kitchens are strange attractors. In the kitchen of my elder daughter, who lives next door to me, there are book-shelves built into every free space, but on top of each top shelf there are piles of books lying horizontally, giving the general effect of a bookshop in Haye-on-Wye. Nev-ertheless, because these women have supervised my latest house since its beginnings, I try to respect their wishes for neatness, which they kindly associate with my comfort. Therefore, in the kitchen-studio which acts as my principal room for reading and writing, the floor-to-ceiling built-in bookcases on either side of the room should take care of my traditional holdings plus any new influx. In practice, however, some nonshelf shelving has appeared. On the kitchen counter, where it meets the wall beside the door, my complete set of Anthony Powell's *A Dance to the Music of Time* stands between a horizontal stack of all the discs of season four of *Game of Thrones*—kindly sent to me by the producers—and another horizontal stack of some of George MacDonald Fraser's *Flashman* novels, not yet read. The *Flashman* novels are popular among my friends and I have always promised myself that I would get around to them. Now that they have invaded my kitchen, they must be dealt with. Elsewhere in the kitchen, on a footlocker beside the couch, a couple of those invisible L-shaped plastic doodads provide support for a vertically arranged display of about half the Patrick O'Brian novels, which look so good in paperback. Thanks to the generous lending policy of my elder daughter and her friend Deirdre Serjeantson—a very learned woman, who is also good for advice on Elizabethan poetic imagery—I had already read the whole Jack Aubrey saga, but when I spotted a bunch of the individual volumes on Hugh's bookstall I thought I had better start my own collection. Madness. Horizontally on the footlocker are also arranged some biographical books about Hemingway. Double madness: they don't even look as if they are standing in a shelf. They just look as if they are lying around.

Upstairs there is a whole floor of the house which has similarly not only been taken over, but where the taking over is being taken over. Most of my books about twentieth-century politics are up there. I sold off my complete set of Martin Gilbert's biography of Churchill, but all of Gilbert's books about World War II and the Holocaust are there. My rationale for this particular cull was that I would be unlikely to find time to read the Churchill biography again, even though one of its volumes, *Finest Hour*, is among the great books about Britain's salvation from barbarism. On the other hand, all six volumes of Churchill's own history of World War II are still there, as if I will have time to pay them another visit. But I probably won't, so their presence is really talismanic. We are often told that the next generation of literati won't have private libraries: everything will be in the computer. It's a rational solution, but that's probably what's wrong with it. Being book crazy is an aspect of love, and therefore scarcely rational at all.

Always Philip Larkin

READING JAMES BOOTH'S cloddishly entitled *Philip Larkin: Life, Art and Love* so that I might review it for the *New York Times Book Review,* I was glad to find that the only sane view of Larkin is once again becoming standard, after too long a period in which there have been serious debates about how so disturbed a psyche could have produced such serenely integrated poetry. (Some pundits resolved the question by announcing that Larkin's poetry was never really much good at all, but luckily their witless views did not penetrate as far as the high schools, where children continued to be told, correctly, that some of Larkin's poems were as good as anything they were ever likely to read.) But for once, while working, I found myself a bit short of the necessary books. Over the years I have accumulated all the individual collections of Larkin's poetry plus both versions of the *Collected Poems* (one version preserves the ordering of the individual volumes while the other version arranges everything chronologically) and I was laboring under the misapprehension that I had enough to go on. Now, reading Booth's treatise, I realized that I needed *The Complete Poems of Philip Larkin,* edited by Archie Burnett. There were scholarly notes to be consulted, and a few poems which I had never seen. Feeling ashamed that there was anything I had missed in the work of a man I had admired so much, I got my personal assistant to press the right buttons on her computer so that Abebooks might supply me with the desired volume. It arrived seemingly within minutes: yet more proof that we have entered a new age. Or, rather, that everyone else has: some of us are leaving too early to get much more than a hint of what life will be like when you will merely have to think of something you want and it will arrive instantly, still crackling with the ozone of the time-space continuum.

By whatever means it was supplied, though, what a glorious book to have on my desk. Promising myself to read only what I needed, I read on and on for hours, even rereading those poems which I have known almost by heart since the week they were first published. (I say "week" because they tended to make their first appearance in such weekly magazines as the *Listener,* whose then editor, Karl Miller, rightly treated the arrival of each fresh Larkin manuscript as a visitation from the angel Gabriel.) During my career as a critic I wrote at least half a dozen articles about Larkin without doing much more than scratching the surface of his brilliance, but I'm sure my instinct was sound in not trying to plumb the depths. The turmoil of his psyche is the least interesting thing about him. His true profundity is right there on the surface, in the beauty of his line. Every ugly moment of his interior battles was in service to that beauty. That being said, his unique thematic originality should be remarked: no other great modern poet, not even Yeats, was so successful at making his own personality the subject, and this despite the fact that his personality was something that he would really rather not have been stuck with. He would rather have been Sidney Bechet.

Villa America

AMANDA VAIL'S 1988 book about Sara and Gerald Murphy, *Everybody Was So Young,* is a disarming treatment of a subject that you have to treat disarmingly or get nowhere. The Murphys brought to Antibes in the 1920s a powerful first taste of the modern American international cocktail of artistic sensitivity and wealth. With prominent Europeans like Picasso eating out of their elegant hands, it was no wonder that the American expatriates—Scott and Zelda Fitzgerald, Hemingway, John Dos Passos, *et hoc genus*—all turned up to enjoy the facilities. The Murphys put some hard work into the Villa America: there were fourteen rooms and seven acres of garden, and the private beach had to be cleared of seaweed. But basically their little empire was an exercise in purchasing power, with the most famous artistic figures of the day included in the inventory. As a star hostess, Sara had the necessary gift of preparing the perfect scene to make it seem effortless. Later on, the golden couple had their tragedies—two children died in sad circumstances—but the basic rhythm of their story was one of stylish leisure, maintained as easily as breathing. Amanda Vail catches the charm. You can see yourself lounging about on the beach and feeling bound to start writing a masterpiece, if not today then tomorrow. Scott Fitzgerald, resenting the fact that the conditions were too good to favor the act of creation, trashed the furniture instead; and Hemingway, unwilling to yield to Gerald the position of center of the action, soon reestablished a due distance.

Fairyland had its tensions. The story has been told before. Calvin Tomkins's 1971 book about the Murphys, *Living Well Is the Best Revenge*, failed to explain its own title (revenge for what? For too big an income?), but it caught the mood. Louis Auchincloss, who knew something about being born to privilege, reviewed Tomkins's book with approval for the way it caught the theme of Sara's dislike of the very idea that Scott Fitzgerald might have based Dick and Nicole in *Tender Is the Night* on her and her husband. Sara resented any suggestion that the ruling couple might have been unhappy. The Murphys had staked their lives on being perfect. Gerald, a painter who gave up painting, probably didn't want to injure his seigneurial role with too much artistic commitment. In retrospect, that can seem a real pity, if you think, as I do, that his paintings were original, with a modern, clean-cut elegance that lasts like the styling of a Cord automobile.

But he wasn't going to let art rule him. He had the means to run his own life, up until the point when catastrophe arrived in the form of arbitrary death for the children. He was able to go back to being a businessman and bury himself behind a desk, but Sara never really recovered. Theirs was a short era, and no dynasty. But their little kingdom generated a specific texture of bliss that was remembered by all who touched it, and by now it is being written about by people who were born long after it was over. You can see how facts might arouse the urge to perpetuate them beyond their time, but it is harder to see why that should be true of flavors and tones. There is a kind of writing that wants us to remember a way of life that the writer never saw. It ought to be a doomed enterprise, yet sometimes it is done well.

Angles on Hitler

HUGH'S BOOKSTALL can sometimes turn into a sort of club. You meet people there who are in the middle of writing a three-volume treatise on the politics of Byzantium. Recently I bumped into Dr. Michael Tanner, a fellow of Corpus Christi who was already one of the smartest minds in the philosophy faculty when I was an undergraduate. He told me that he was under strict instruction to bring no more books into his house, so he had to smuggle them in and hide them. Since I was under something like the same embargo myself, it was clearly time to sit down at a coffee bar and discuss the protocols and techniques of book-smuggling. Tanner is generally informed about the arts to a daunting level, but he is also very funny, and I soon had to tacitly concede that his imitation of Elizabeth Schwarzkopf teaching a master class was better than mine. (To illustrate her drawbacks as a teacher, you have to be able to evoke what her mouth looked like when she sang an umlaut: she looked as if she were trying to kiss the behind of a hummingbird in midflight.) Mention of the famous soprano's early career in Nazi Berlin led us naturally to the eternal subject of Hitler's interest in the arts. Tanner contended, in the nicest possible way, that *Hitler and the Power of Aesthetics*, by Frederic Spotts, was an essential book on this subject. He had correctly guessed that I hadn't read it. I wrote away for it and soon found this to be true. Spotts gives Hitler all the credit he could possibly have coming for a range of cultural interests that was wider than we tend to think. Certainly his passion for music, or anyway for opera, extended far beyond Wagner and Lehar: he also liked Puccini and Verdi, and could tell you about them as he could tell you about everything.

But I still feel that there is a danger of underestimating one of Hitler's most demonic gifts: he had the con-man's knack of making himself seem profoundly steeped in any subject just by the fluency with which he could learn a list of facts and reel them off to the susceptible ear of a worshiping disciple. There were Wehrmacht officers, some of them high up in the business of commissioning new weapons, who were amazed by how much Hitler knew about tanks. But what he knew about tanks was a pastiche of stuff he had picked up from random study, and to the extent that his policies on armaments were carried out, they ensured the loss of the war. It seems a logical inference that many of the artistic subjects he touched on in conversation he knew more fleetingly than he made it sound. I have always found it hard to believe Hitler's claim, which Spotts unquestioningly repeats, that he carried the five volumes of Schopenhauer's collected works in his knapsack throughout his time in the trenches. I have those five volumes on my shelves, and they make quite a weight even in a thin-paper edition. But there can be no doubt about Hitler's aesthetic passion: Spotts is dead right about that. Hitler was up all night studying Speer's scale model of a future Berlin while the actual Berlin was being pounded to pieces around his ears. As can so easily happen for a man in trouble, art was an escape route.

While Martin Amis was preparing the manuscript of his novel *The Zone of Interest*, he caught me out in correspondence when I had to confess that I had not read Ron Rosenbaum's *Explaining Hitler*. I bought it, read it at the table in my kitchen, and was suitably impressed. Rosenbaum does a good job of balancing up the central theses of the two main postwar interpreters of Hitler's personality: Hugh Trevor-Roper and Alan Bullock. Trevor-Roper, in his worldwide best seller *The Last Days of Hitler,* thought that Hitler did indeed possess a mysterious, charismatic secret: how else could he have still been obeyed when all his real power was gone? Bullock, in *Hitler: A Study in Tyranny,* thought that Hitler was a mountebank. Later on, Bullock took a second position, calling Hitler an actor who believed in his own act. The two professors were both on the case early (in the German cities the *Trümmerwelt,* the world of ruins, was still being cleared away), but between them they caught the Hitler story better than the supposedly major studies did later on: I haven't read Joachim Fest's Hitler biography since it came out in 1974, but lately I have slogged my way through Ian Kershaw's massive two-volume effort (he is a thorough writer without being an attractive one), and I couldn't find much that Trevor-Roper and Bullock didn't catch more than half a century back. I must read Trevor-Roper and Bullock again. When I first read them I was still in my teens, and they helped to form my view of life, but old men forget. Sometimes slightly younger men get things wrong, however: Rosenbaum was born in 1946, so perhaps he has not quite had time to pick up the odd item of seemingly incidental, but in fact vital, information. When he says that the prewar newsreels were "speeded up," and that this "jerkiness" contributed to the robotized atmospherics of Nazi maneuvers, he is making a false point. At the time they were filmed, prewar newsreels didn't look speeded up, because they were projected at the correct rate. Later on, the rate changed. As a general rule, writers should be wary about making technical points.

Stephen Edgar, Australian Ace

MY FRIEND Stephen Edgar is the supreme lyricist among the current wave of Australian poets. Les Murray is the acknowledged master, the Magister Illyrio in our Free City of Pentos—here I attempt to forecast one of the *Game of Thrones* allusions that might be standard usage among the cultural critics of the generation to come—and I suppose that in the long run all of us will be measured by our distance from him. But others can do strikingly individual things: Peter Goldsworthy, for example, can actually write in the tiny, haiku-like measures that everyone admires but hardly anyone can handle; and Judith Beveridge, with her uncanny powers of observation and evocation, is unbeatable when it comes to portraying nature as only marginally needing humans. And there are more. But nobody, not even Murray, can put an intricate form together like Stephen Edgar. Swiss watches aren't in the race, especially now that all they contain is a microprocessor and a battery. The typical Edgar poem generates an astonishing first force from its panscopic wealth of imagery, and then that force is multiplied by the way it is put together, with verse paragraphs that flow meticulously from stanza to stanza, and every stanza a new formal discovery in itself. I have all his books, and today his new book arrives: *Exhibits of the Sun.*

Just the thing to take with me on this afternoon's visit to the Infusion Suite at Addenbrooke's, where, once every three weeks, I sit for a whole afternoon with a tube plugged into my arm. As what seem gallons of immunoglobulin are pumped through the tube, I am going nowhere. It is an ideal time for reading, but the book has to be the right size, so as not to demand too much handling, lest my cannula get joggled loose. (In that idea can be heard an incipient poem, which might be comic; as, indeed, is the whole process. I feel like Iron Man in the repair shop.) Quite soon I plan to make a start on Conrad's *Victory,* but for this afternoon I have Stephen Edgar's new volume.

As always, perfection is Edgar's territory. A typical poem by him leaves nothing more to say, nor any other way of saying it. His poem about Walter Benjamin's famous angel of history—the angel that flies backward with its vision full of accumulating ruins—gives us a picture of the ruins: "one vast / Impacted havoc." But even more remarkably, it also gives us the angel's feelings, how "he longs to stay" but is forever swept onward: "a storm is blowing out of Paradise." These phrases do Benjamin even more honor by quoting him directly: but their placing is all Edgar's. Savoring a hundred moments like that, as President Reagan might have binged on a packet of Jelly Belly Super Sours, I reflect on how far the Australian cultural expansion has come. And so it should have done: Australia has twice the population of Sweden, which gave the world Saab, Volvo, and Abba. (The third conglomerate made more money than the first two put together.) But Australia remains a small country. It just looks big on the map. Any feelings of isolation that its intelligentsia once had, however, no longer fit the facts. Its film directors and actors, its singers and conductors, are everywhere. The theater director Michael Blakemore has several times had hit shows running in London and New York both at once. Even in poetry, a field which has no real commercial existence, there is an

Australian presence in the world. Once, as recently as in the previous generation, this was not so, and there was a justifiable niggling ache from the marginalization. But now the Australian poets don't have to waste their time thinking on nationalist lines at all, because the world is their oyster. I never expected this to happen in my time. It should be no surprise, however: along with the freedom to prosper, the freedom to create is one of the first freedoms a democracy offers. And even the Americans now know roughly where Australia is. All over the world, any underprivileged or oppressed group of people would like to get into Australia. Though many are invited in—for its intake of immigrants, Australia rates high as a host nation—they can't all come: a fact which gives the Australian pseudo-left intellectuals, always looking for a new grievance, a chance to call their own country an offense to mankind. Meanwhile the first container ship full of Australian Aboriginals has yet to arrive in the Persian Gulf. As I reflect on these things, I resolve to take down from the shelf, this very night, Stephen Edgar's nearest thing to a definitive selection—published in the United States, it is called *The Red Sea*—and further soothe my aching brain. Along with my heart, my brain is practically the last part of me that works, but the news from the Middle East is enough to further scarify the mental lesions one already has. A new group of extremist killers has shown up who regard Al-Qaeda as being too soft on the infidel. A storm is blowing out of Paradise.

John Howard Extends His Reign

I GAVE JOHN HOWARD's hulking autobiography *Laz-arus Rising* to my younger daughter for a birthday present, and now I have borrowed it back. She was impressed, and I am too. Prime minister of Australia for more than eleven and a half years, Howard was never a physically impos-ing figure. When he went out for a run every morning, he could leave some of the journalists gasping, but show-ing off was not his style. He writes as he spoke: always clear but never exciting. To be without style was his style: on holidays at Nambucca Heads on the northern coast of New South Wales, he would paddle about in the water in his long shorts with a hat improvised out of a handker-chief to protect him from the sun. At such times he was the very picture of what Australians call the Aussie Battler: the average bloke slogging along to keep his family fed and well. But in Parliament his mind came into play, and it ran rings around the opposition, the Australian Labor Party, or ALP. The ALP regarded him as the devil. So did almost the whole of the Australian intelligentsia, who have been handing down their elementary anti-American, anticapitalist, and indeed anti-Australian views from one generation to the next for many years now. There is a vestigial blue-collar left to which I myself still belong, but the much more vocal white-collar left has always been united in hating Howard, despite, or perhaps because of, his popularity with the electorate. The Labor Party spent a doomed decade looking for a leader who would be so different from Howard that the electorate would change its allegiance. Then Kevin Rudd realized that the only way to win against Howard was to promise to do all the same things Howard did, but do them younger.

Howard's book is an educational text for showing how far you can get in Australian politics by balancing the books and saying what you mean. Nevertheless, he could make mistakes, and he made a whopping mistake in his last term, when he somehow concluded that he could not endorse his highly competent treasurer, Peter Costello, as his natural successor. Effectively, Howard was calling himself indispensable. The British have a monarch anyway; and the Americans treat their president as a monarch, some-times with ludicrously overblown results; but most Aus-tralians want no monarchies any closer than, say, London.

I deduce from Howard's book, which is luminously self-aware in all other respects, that Howard never quite grasped why he was toppled. But the answer is not beyond analysis: as long as he behaved as if he thought of himself as an ordinary man, intelligent voters were ready to think him extraordinary, but when he behaved as if he thought of himself as an extraordinary man, he was finished.

Finished but not quite. He has written this book, and soon there will be another one about the Menzies era. The name of Menzies, crucial to modern Australian history, is already forgotten out there in the less fortunate world, and soon the name of Howard will be too, to anyone except a student of Western democracy. But he's ready for that.

One of the many admirable things about him was that he genuinely believed that to be prime minster of Aus-tralia was quite enough glory to be going on with. His successor, Kevin Rudd, wanted to be secretary general of the United Nations. The debate goes on about which of Howard's successors was worse: Kevin Rudd or Julia Gil-lard. To help scramble the question further, each of these two Labor Party giants has published a book vilifying the other. In the meanwhile, Howard is adding to the essential literature which will help explain to the next generation of Australians just how their nation has come to hold its exceptional position.

Hemingway at the End

STARTING WITH Carlos Baker's pioneering biography in 1969, called simply *Hemingway*, I have spent a good part of my adult life reading books about Ernest Hemingway, and I don't want to die among a heap of them, but they keep getting into the house. Once, there were people who wrote books about Hemingway who were born after he became famous. By now there are people who write books about Hemingway who were born after he killed himself. Some of these scholars, back in the old days, were professors of American literature in general before they switched full time to Hemingway. Nowadays they tend to spend their entire careers in Hemingway studies. Whether yesterday or today, their common qualification is the ability to produce yet another book about Hemingway, sometimes including a whole new fact.

In my experience, even if you don't read these books

about Hemingway, you will own half a dozen of them. I suppose I keep reading them for the same reason that people can't help writing them: he's too much of a problem to leave unsolved. Beside Hemingway, even d'Annunzio is a mere zany. Hemingway's personality was so extravagant that his creative work occupied only a small corner of it. In some ways, that fact was a blessing. He was never driven back to mere aestheticism when searching for material. He could measure his manhood by how he shot and fished. Unfortunately, he also measured his manhood by how he wrote. It wasn't enough for him to prove his bravery by shooting a charging lion or blasting at sharks with a tommy gun to preserve the carcass of the giant marlin he had just finished fighting after a whole day in the chair. He wanted us to admire the bravery with which he rewrote his latest manuscript for the 323rd time. For a figure like that, we only had his word for it, and he could get very angry— fighting angry—if anybody suggested that he was making anything up. Honesty and accuracy were masculine things.

But in his case, perhaps in everybody's case, his sexuality was of a dual nature. Thus his pose of masculinity was in opposition to his sensitivity. This gap in his mental makeup as a writer he tried to weld shut with style. To some extent he succeeded, especially early on, and even when he didn't succeed he wielded a pervasive influence. The style was a virus. Younger would-be writers took it as the sound of truth, of real experience lived and assimilated. The facts say that he was at his most persuasive when making things up. One of the most lastingly famous scenes in *A Farewell to Arms* is usually called the Retreat from Caporetto. A long and dazzling tour de force, it has the same stamp of authenticity as a short story like "Big Two-Hearted River." But Hemingway never saw the Retreat from Caporetto. It happened the year before he got to Italy. He simply had the gift of turning a few facts he had read or heard about into a convincing narrative. He could do the same with a few lies. His way of putting things was a transformative illusion.

As such, it could bind any acolyte with a spell. I have just finished reading Paul Hendrickson's *Hemingway's Boat*, the story of the close relationship, stretching from 1934 to 1961, between the great writer and his fishing launch, the *Pilar*, which, operating out of Key West and Cuba, carried its owner to his adventures with the big fish and the German submarines. (The fish existed, but about the submarines he could only claim to have provided valuable information about their location: i.e., there weren't any.) The book is a solid seven hundred pages and I read them all, but I don't begrudge the time. Hendrickson has a good, hard head, and tracks down every exaggeration. Nor is he floored by the consideration that Hemingway should never have needed to exaggerate. No doubt there is the occasional maddened dwarf who dreams of being a giant, but Hemingway was a giant who dreamed of being a giant. Years ago, on my first trip to Cuba, in the days when Castro was still making speeches that could be measured in geological time, I was given a tour of the Finca Vigía and saw the *Pilar* up on its blocks. You weren't allowed in the house because the floorboards were giving way, but you could look through the window and marvel at his walls of books. There, on the floor, was a pair of his moccasins. They were like two canoes side by side. The man was from Brobdingnag.

But even though Hendrickson prides himself on getting Hemingway's number, he can't help being infected by the style. When Hemingway beats his chest and boasts that he wrote good, Hendrickson forgets to note that for any lesser writer to echo such bombast even faintly is a guarantee that he will write bad. Still, Hendrickson's brain survived his encounter with Hemingway's, which was clearly in a dreadful mess long before he ended the agony with a shotgun.

Kenneth S. Lynn's 1991 full-length biography of *Hemingway* is another seven hundred–page whopper. Less infected with Papa-style would-be factual posturing, it is even more depressing, because it removes any trust you might have had that Hemingway got sick slowly. Alas, he was in trouble from the beginning. Like Rilke he was raised as a girl by a doting, perhaps slightly mad, mother. He spent his truncated lifetime ridden with doubts about his sexual nature that not even his world-beating pose as an athlete and animal killer could cure. Alcohol couldn't cure them either. His intake of booze is practically the saddest thing about him, because it became evident, quite early on, that he couldn't drink at that rate without pickling his brains. Beside him, a mere lush like William Faulkner sounds like a teetotaler. Strangely enough, we tend to think of Scott Fitzgerald as the juice-head, and Hemingway as the man of discipline. When Hemingway, in "The Snows of Kilimanjaro," wrote those fateful three words "Poor Scott Fitzgerald," he helped to weaken his rival's profile for generations to come. Such is the power of images transmitted posthumously through the media: in actuality, Hemingway was the drinker beyond redemption. But he was so talented, and so masterful at projecting his masculine image, that the impression he gave of being the man in control has lasted all the way until now, and will probably last forever.

There is something to it. Dwight Macdonald was correct to point out that the mannerisms of *The Old Man and the Sea* go all the way back to the first, supposedly disciplined, stories: but underneath the fussy surface of overwrought simplicity there is a lasting strength of visualization. It wasn't his alone—D. H. Lawrence was just as good at describing a clear stream in a mountain valley—but Hemingway had the most of it, and in a way you couldn't miss. He made a thing of it, as young people say.

Unfortunately, to descend another layer, underneath the lasting strength there is an incurable weakness. The duality in his sexual nature was something that he could never explore directly, but only through hints. For the writer who defied all other limitations, his own inner life was taboo. The height of his tragedy was that he could not write about his own finale, which, lasting so long, could have been his great theme. For any writer who does not die instantly, the time of physical decline is a new subject. But he would have been in no condition to tackle it even had he felt free. Too many injuries to the head had wrecked his concentration. He would stand there blasting away at his Royal Quiet DeLuxe (he wrote standing up), typing the same sentence over and over, actually producing the numberless drafts that he had once only boasted of. But even had he been in physical shape, he was psychologically proof against what he would have needed: an honesty that might have been taken as weakness by the media parasites that he had been too afraid of to ward off. His only way out was to destroy himself. He should have had aesthetic objections to that. It left a terrible mess, which his loved ones, to whom he knew he had been a burden, had to clean up. It was ungallant of him, and it wasn't brave. A measure of his magnificence, however, is that we feel so sorry.

On Wit

MARINA TSVETAEVA said that Boris Pasternak, in his youth, looked like an Arab *and* his horse. The underlining of a single word is the stroke of wit. I was thinking of the economical nature of wit—if a sentence is wordy, then it's never witty—when I was once again reading Abba Eban's *Personal Witness,* one of his essential books on the history of Israel, the state that he did so much to bring into being. Nobody in the world was more learned than Eban: his triple first from Cambridge was in three hard ancient languages, and he was conversationally fluent in several of the modern languages as well. (When he was Israel's ambassador to the United Nations, delegates from Arab nations seated on each side of him had long conversations across his back until they finally caught on that he understood everything they were saying.) But there have been learned men who have been unable to keep things brief.

Eban could do with a prose idea what the poet must learn
to do with a poetic idea: make it mark out a space and then
fill that space exactly. Of a U.N. official he could not admire, Eban said that he was a man of few words, but they
were enough to express his range of ideas. I can't think of
a niftier way of putting that. Eban knew how to throttle
back on the witticisms, however, or he would never have
been the great orator he was. The audience for a serious
speech is there to listen to the deep fire of reason, not to the
crackle of a Las Vegas stand-up act. Lately, after reading
both *Personal Witness* and *Abba Eban: An Autobiography*
again, I ordered *Voice of Israel* on the web. It is a collection
of Eban's speeches, many of them of historic moment.
Dealing with the most serious subjects conceivable in his
world, up to and including the possible obliteration of the
nation he represented, they are light on laughs, but always
impressively compact. Off the record, he could be funny
even about the stuff of tragedy. Eban was the man who
said that Yasser Arafat never missed an opportunity to miss
an opportunity. The crack contained, compressed into a
few atoms, everything that spelled tragedy for the Pales-
tinian refugees. The Israelis survived Arafat's leadership,
but for the Palestinians it was a straight stretch downhill

all the way to Hamas, whose rule in Gaza has been such a conspicuous part of the great international political disaster that marks the end of my time on earth. How good it would be to be sure that the nightmare will not stretch on into the next generation. But of course it will.

Richard Wilbur's Precept

DURING THE LONG and taxing business of preparing the text of my *Poetry Notebook* for publication, I deliberately did not look at the great American poet Richard Wilbur's book of critical prose, which I have been reading, off and on, ever since it came out in 1976. I was too afraid of echoing his tone, and of seeming servile if I did so. But I couldn't fail to remember his knack for laying out his knowledge in an easy-seeming sweep of conversational English. (How did literary theory get started? Because the theorists couldn't write.) Several of my touchstone poets—Larkin, Auden, and Eliot would be other examples—had the gift of talking with a passionate detachment about the art they practiced, but I always thought that Wilbur was the kingpin. Now I can safely read his prose again; and find that his chapter "Poetry's Debt to Poetry" still strikes me as the ideal lesson, for beginning students, in how to think about the way the poetic heritage is handed down through the generations. Without a conscious display of erudition, but with a wealth of solid knowledge learned by heart, he gives you the sense that all the poets who have ever mattered always knew about any poet who mattered before them, even if they did not approve. (If the question had been raised of how Dante could have made Homer king of all the poets without being able to read him, Wilbur would have had the answer: Dante could not read Homer, but he trusted Virgil's opinion.) It was in this essay that Wilbur crystallized the formulation that has stayed with me so usefully ever since: in poetry, all the revolutions are palace revolutions.

That being said, ignorance can have, within strict limits, a creative power of its own. With all my critical writing about poetry done and dusted, I really didn't want to discover any new poets, so I was almost glad to know nothing about Richard Howard. But only almost. Having now discovered him—through his rich collection *Inner Voices*—I am impressed by his long lifetime of work in verse. Born in 1929, he has ten years on me and has always used his time to lyrical and learned effect, even when writing criticism; so how can I, of all people, have not known he was there? Like the leading pair of my other formalist Americans, Richard Wilbur and Anthony Hecht, he has the gift of working a mind-ful of memories and impressions into an apprehensible shape.

Had I encountered Richard Howard early on, I might even have been affected in my own poetry by the sheer delight he takes in spreading his erudition through a stanza. To take only one example, his poem "Venetian Interior, 1889," might be subtitled "All you need to know about what happened to Robert Browning's son." It is a sumptuous piece of work, a boutique with the range of a supermarket. But it also runs on. Brevity is not in his gift, or anyway not among his interests: he presumes his readers have the time. In my own work I have always assumed that the readers have no time at all, and need their attention snared from moment to moment, even when I am translating the *Divine Comedy*. But on that point, reassurance comes from Dante himself: in the *Inferno* he always has a new event waiting around every corner, and in his *Paradiso* there is another light show every ten minutes. Still, Richard Howard's relaxed approach has its virtues.

Above all, he has a better reason for writing than merely to be recognized. In that regard, it would be conceited on my part to think that he ever needed my approval. Such a conceit is a *déformation professionnelle* for critics: after an initial period of relative sanity, they tend to think that nothing—not even the career of, say, Horace—ever happened without their interest in it. At its worst, the madness reaches the point where the critic behaves as if his new book about Shakespeare will save Shakespeare from oblivion. One way of praising Richard Howard would be to say that his mentality is the exact opposite: the note of nonpossessive appreciation is one that he strikes with every sentence he writes, and when it shows up in a poem it has a bewitching effect, even when the poem is ten times longer than the complete works of Samuel Menashe.

So, come to think of it, I am doubly glad that I didn't find Richard Howard earlier, but found him only now, when the pleasure of discovery can no longer pose any difficult choices. Wilbur might have added one further thought to his famous precept: all the revolutions are palace revolutions, but there is the occasional klutz who never figures out what's going on until it's all over.

And goddam it, I have just found another accomplished and erudite American poet, in the books section of the

Oxfam shop near Magdalene bridge: Lawrence Joseph. His collection *Codes, Precepts, Biases, and Taboos* is full of quotable lines. I deduce from his Wikipedia entry (his book's biographical note is coy about this information, as if he were a female film star) that he was born nine years after me, so where have I been all his life? And Stephen Edgar, in a letter, has only just now mentioned the name of the late Edgar Bowers, who turns out to have been an American formalist poet who not only came out of World War II like Richard Wilbur and Anthony Hecht but wrote poems intricate and precise enough to be considered along with theirs. I'm supposed to rest content with a comprehensive viewpoint marinated in experience, not to be jolted out of my bed-socks every five minutes by the belated discovery of someone who has been toiling away impeccably for decades writing exactly the sort of thing I have so often proclaimed indispensable. Further evidence, here, for a bittersweet truth: any overview of the cultural world, like any system of mathematics, can't be complete without being false. We can legitimately preen ourselves on being brighter than the next literary critic down the corridor, but we had better not imagine that we are brighter than Gödel.

But I must put Lawrence Joseph aside, because I have a new poem on the way, and it is always fatal, I have found, when you have something of your own to write, to get too close to someone else's music. It gets into your lungs like secondary smoking.

When Creation Is Perverse

AS THE BRITISH PRISONS continue to fill up with vet-
eran showbiz luminaries who have been busted for some
sexual perversion with which they created emotional
havoc in the days of their physical strength, I give thanks
that my own compulsions were legal. An artist's work is
harder to like when it turns out that his sexual proclivities
were criminal. Nevertheless, on the principle that fine art
is usually the work of flawed people, one strives to maintain one's appreciation. Eric Gill's work I don't much care
about, so there is no problem in wishing it all to the devil
along with him. But Adolf Loos designed perfect coffee-
houses, and Peter Altenberg wrote perfect paragraphs:
I find it hard to imagine the texture of a Vienna without their work. Balthus remains a real problem, because
so many of his pictures haunt the memory, although it
should have been obvious at the moment the memories got

started that the pictures were perverse. For a long while
I thought Basil Bunting was no problem at all: his taste
for barely pubescent girls showed up in his poetry, but his
poetry had nothing else in it. Lately, however, I have been
reading his *Collected Poems* of 1970 (an Oxfam discovery),
and I find that I was wrong all along. Whole stretches of
his strangely crowded, clotted, and jagged verse are quite
marvelous. Some of his notorious echoes of Ezra Pound
are better than the originals. (If Bunting's phrase "stork's
stilts cleaving sun-disk" had appeared in Pound's *Cantos*,
academics would have written articles about it.) Yet this
inventive and dedicated man was every father's nightmare.
The best one can say for him is that he will live on, if he
does, in the same category as Balthus: producers of images
that you are glad to have in your head, even though their
own heads were nests of vipers. The provenance of art can
never be as morally elementary as we wish it. Art grows
from the world, and the world, as Louis MacNeice said,
is incorrigibly plural. This cruel but consoling fact really
shows up when you start the slide to nowhere. The air is
lit by a shimmering tangle of all the reasons you are sad to
go and all the reasons you are glad to leave. It's the glow
of life: apparently simple, yet complex beyond analysis.

Nevertheless, morality continues to send its strong interior signal that it is either absolute or it is nothing. Bill Cosby's jokes used to make me laugh so much that years later I would laugh again when I remembered them. Today the laughter comes less easily. If he turns out to be guilty, how will we take back our appreciation? Ours is a minor problem, however, when compared with his.

Conrad's Greatest Victory

STARTING IN THE infusion suite at the hospital, and continuing as I Ambulate up and down my kitchen, I have been reading Conrad's *Victory;* and I feel that my recent years of reading have come to a kind of culmination. First published in 1915, the novel perfects Conrad's signature themes. The hero, Heyst, is a Lord Jim figure without the guilt. Heyst has managed to get beyond the bounds of civilization, and even of capitalism: the coal company that he helped to found in the islands has fallen into ruins, but he himself has survived. In the dance hall of the despicable hotelier Schomberg, Heyst encounters the ideal girl, Alma, who is the helpless prisoner of the tatty Zangiacomo Orchestra and has nowhere to turn as Schomberg odiously threatens her with his attentions. Heyst bears her away to Samburan, a magic kingdom like Patusan and Sulaco. There, seemingly in control of events, he calls her

Lena, princess of Samburan. They are like Adam and Eve, needing only each other. Or so it seems: but it soon emerges that they need a knowledge of evil, too, because it is heading toward them in the chilling form of "plain Mr. Jones," one of Conrad's most profound studies in terror. As the collision between bliss and destruction gets closer, the reader will spend at least a hundred pages praying that Heyst has a gun hidden away somewhere. The first big slaughterhouse battles of the Great War had already been fought while Conrad was publishing the novel, but there is not a hint of pacifism. Conrad knew that unarmed goodwill is useless against armed malice. It was to be a lesson that the coming century would teach over and over, and so on into the present century: peace is not a principle, it is only a desirable state of affairs, and can't be obtained without a capacity for violence at least equal to the violence of the threat. Conrad didn't want to reach this conclusion any more than we do, but his artistic instincts were proof against the slightest tinge of mystical spiritual solace, and so should ours be. Our age of massacres has also been an age of the intellectual charlatan, when people claiming to interpret events can barely be relied upon to give a straightforward account of what actually happened.

Conrad was the writer who reached political adulthood before any of the other writers of his time, and when they did, they reached only to his knee.

That being said, however, it must be admitted that Heyst's upright stupidity grows tedious in the final scenes. Conrad should have made his heroes as intelligent as himself, the better to illustrate his thematic concern with how the historic forces that crush the naïve will do the same to the wise, if they do not prepare to fight back. Finally, he tends to reinforce our wishful thought that cultivation—gained, for example, from reading the novels of Joseph Conrad—might be enough to ward off barbarism. But barbarism doesn't care if we are cultivated or not.

Coda

I HAVE BEEN READING two biographies at once. One, Lucy Hughes-Hallett's *The Pike,* which is the life story of Gabriele d'Annunzio, deals with an almost entirely worthless individual: he wrote some resounding poetry, but otherwise he was good for nothing except whipping crowds into protofascist hysteria and proving that a galloping case of halitosis was no hindrance to his uncanny success with women. He must have had something, or so distinguished a woman as Eleonora Duse would not have gone to bed with him: but on the whole the only reason you would want to raise the raving twerp from his grave would be so that you could slap his face. The other biography is Mark Bostridge's *Florence Nightingale,* the story of one of the most worthwhile individuals in the world. I am trying to do my duty to justice by finding her more interesting than him. On the plane of brute fact, nothing could be more interesting than how D'Annunzio, after the Paris premiere of Diaghilev's *Cleopatra*, insinuated himself into Ida Rubinstein's crowded dressing room and crammed his face between her legs. In sharp contrast, the only scandal generated by Florence Nightingale was the kind of brain-dead press concoction familiar to us today: in the hospital at Scutari, she watched amputations to learn how the process could be made less traumatic, and the press took the opportunity of calling her a sadist.

She was, of course, exactly the opposite thing. Mercy was her vocation. That being said, her preoccupation was to take the practical steps that would transform nursing into an act of public benevolence, with a set of procedures to be universally instilled. The inertia that she had to overcome being nearly as powerful as a whole society, she had no time for mere fine feelings.

From Bostridge's exemplary book, a heartening impression emerges of how Nightingale could think on a vast scale while never shifting her attention from the importance of detail. Much of her reforming zeal was prescient. A germ theory of disease was still a quarter of a century in the future, but she somehow realized the vital role that could be played by cleanliness. Thus she transformed the Scutari hospital from a hellhole into a refuge. Her distinction of mind marks every chapter of her story, even those chapters which occurred before she saw what her true role was. She was greatly gifted in languages, in statistics, in conversation, in music, in learning, and in all the arts of civilization. She was full of fun. In the thinking of the day—it was still the thinking only yesterday—she would have made some brilliant man the perfect wife. But she guessed, correctly, that she was cut out for something more. Richard Monckton Milnes was a clever and charming man, but she turned him down. In the movie, starring Jaclyn Smith (fresh from her triumphs as one of *Charlie's Angels*), *he* turns *her* down. But the movie isn't as silly as you might think, because to portray Florence Nightingale as a beauty was not all that implausible. She was very attractive, and was well capable of being attracted to the right man. But she was even more attracted to a life lived on her own account, in service to a principle. It was a life that helped give us the hospital systems that we know today, and to give nurses the respect they deserve.

Nurses are on my mind of late. At Addenbrooke's I see them all the time, and I expect the day will soon come when I see almost nobody else. Bless them all, of all colors and creeds. Just after I first got ill, and while I was waiting for my prostate operation, I was wearing my urinary tract externally, in an arrangement featuring a catheter plus a hefty plastic bag taped to my leg. Or anyway it was hefty when it was full. One night the bag broke and suddenly the floor was awash with amber piss. I signaled the night nurse, who told me to stop apologizing. (In such circumstances, I have found, one tends to apologize for one's mere existence.) She set about mopping it up. She had a deformed body, with limbs all the wrong lengths. Life could never have been easy for her. But now she was making the end of life easier for me. It was a night to remember, and I haven't forgotten it for a second. I can only hope that the sum total of my writings has been as useful to the world as her kindness, but I doubt that this is so.

After a series of cataract operations I am left with one eye working, and I sometimes wonder what would happen to my reading if that one began to shut down too. Meanwhile, I am already getting some practice at inhabiting the web world, where nothing is supposed to go on for too long. The excellent American poet Dan Brown has started posting a set of short critical analyses on his blog: a poem by his hero George Herbert, for instance, is made subject to an intense and knowledgeable technical analysis, only a paragraph or two long. Clearly Dan Brown is ready to use this compressed form to discuss any poetic mystery except why he still calls himself Dan Brown. In view of the fact that the perpetrator of best-selling thrillers of only semi–mental merit is already called Dan Brown, and that the name is therefore famous even in, say, Thailand, you would expect that Dan Brown the poet might at least call himself Dan M. Brown, if not Denzil Hercules Bairnsfeather III. But no, there he is, still writing exquisite metaphysical poetry under a name that might as well be Jerry Lewis. That's not the point here, however. The point is that to read his latest critical thought I didn't have to limp out into the cold or even dial up a bookshop on the web. I just had to tap in his name. This is the next world arriving.

I don't quite believe that in the era of the web every piece of writing should be short. I wouldn't want a short version of *War and Peace*. But there are already literary periodicals that make a thing of shortness, as if written specifically for people who are bright but tired. My elder daughter has just introduced me to *Slightly Foxed*. Numbers appear regularly, and are full of short pieces about books that vanished, or that should be better known. Perhaps already falling into that classification myself, I tour each issue, lighting on articles when I know the name. A recent issue has an excellent piece about *Alamein to Zem Zem*, the fugitive little volume produced by Keith Douglas when he was fighting in the western desert. Later on he got killed in Normandy, just after D-Day. He was a superbly gifted poet who would have changed the state of the art had he lived, but he was cut short. One is lucky to have lived this long. There is a love poem from Douglas, called "Canoe," and an elegy called "Vergissmeinicht." He could point at them and say: if I'd had the chance, I would have done a lot more of that.

Now we must do the pointing for him. My idea of criticism's duty is somewhere in that obligation. The critic should write to say, not "look how much I've read," but "look at this, it's wonderful." If the young feel compelled to come and see your tomb, there should be something good written on it. Here in Cambridge, in Trinity College Chapel, there is a plaque dedicated to Ludwig Wittgenstein. It says, in Latin, that he released thought from its bonds in language. If I ever had a plaque, I would like it to say: He loved the written word, and told the young.

I speak as one whose languages are disappearing. Soon,

I suppose, only English will be left, and then not even that. But if, at last, the written word retreats out of reach, what then? I am not much of a one for audio books, unless they are read by their own authors. Unfortunately, too many of them are read by actors. On the whole I hate the way actors read, always running on through the punctuation as if their task was to turn written forms into dialogue. One of them, I name no names, read my poem "Japanese Maple" aloud on the air in Australia just after it came out in the *New Yorker*. His voice was majestic, but he had no intention of observing the line endings and stanza breaks, which he took as an interference with his gift for naturalism. I tuned in on the web to listen, and felt that I had been tied to a chair and beaten up by Basil Rathbone.

My younger daughter and I could always watch *Band of Brothers* again, not to mention the whole of *The West Wing* from start to finish. If my weakening eyesight missed a plot point, she could explain it to me; as she quite often has to do already. The dialogue of *The Newsroom*, written by Aaron Sorkin, is often too fast for me and my wife, but not too fast for either of our daughters, who are in a continual state of supplying us with an English version of Sorkinese, like simultaneous translators at the United Nations. Coping with the output of the modern media can be a group effort, thereby lending substance to Proust's wonderful idea about the community of minds. Usually it takes a whole bunch of us to understand anything, so anyone who thinks he can do the whole thing by himself is almost certainly a crackpot. Probably even Richard Feynman occasionally needed to have something explained to him. He was the kind of theoretical physicist who could actually fix your telephone, but I wish he'd lived to hear Josh and Donna in *The West Wing* simultaneously delivering a page of dialogue each in half a minute. Quantum mechanics might have struck him as a cinch compared with that.

And then, there is music. At least one of my doctors thinks I need music in order to heal. Alas, the truth is that music has never soothed me. I just find it too interesting. I should be listening to the late Beethoven quartets, and those two lovely quintets by Mozart, all the time; but I would get nothing read or written, because great music was never designed to be played in the background. If it moves to the foreground, I will be on my way out at last. I will be halfway through the dazzling, multifaceted wall of books, and on the brink of nothingness, where everything begins again, but for different people.